Quilting with Jodie in COTTON COUNTRY

Jodie Davis with Jayne Davis

Breckling Press

Library of Congress Cataloging-in-Publication Data

Davis, Jodie,
   Quilting with Jodie in cotton country / Jodie Davis with Jayne Davis.
     p. cm.
  ISBN 1-933308-05-2
   1. Appliqué—Patterns. 2. Quilting—Patterns. I. Davis, Jayne S. II.
Title.

   TT779.D3794 2006
   746.46′041—dc22

2006022805

Editorial direction by Anne Knudsen
Cover and interior design by Bartko Design
Cover and interior photographs by Sharon Hoogstraten
Hand drawings by Iia Owens-Williams
Technical drawings by Kathryn Wager Wright

This book was set in Minion Pro, Clarendon, and Trade Gothic by Bartko Design, Inc.

Published by Breckling Press
283 N. Michigan St, Elmhurst, IL 60126

Printed and bound in China
International Standard Book Number: 1-933308-05-2 (ISBN 13: 978-1-933308-05-2)

Contents

Welcome to Cotton Country

A QUILTER'S FABRIC STASH is her most precious possession, so take a trip with me to the very heart of the quilting experience, where home-grown cotton is ginned into fabric. Come, the cotton fields beckon.

Across the Southern states of Alabama, Arkansas, Georgia, Louisiana, Mississippi, and the Carolinas, the late summer fields are abloom with soft white cotton. Sweeping as far north as Virginia and west to Oklahoma and even California, cotton is still king. Starting in Louisiana and Georgia, I took a trip through Cotton Country. I followed the amazing—and lengthy—process of turning raw cotton into printed fabric. I immersed myself in both the way Southern farm life is and the way it once was. Along the way, I got to know the people whose lives are devoted to each of the many magical transformations cotton undergoes as it makes its journey from the field to the quilt shop.

As a Yankee, I quickly learned that my pre-conceptions of the traditional South were not quite accurate. Yes, there are large plantations, but most, such as Frogmore Plantation in Frogmore, Louisiana, are modest in size and every family member works—hard—to keep everything running smoothly. Family farms are, I discovered, the norm, growing food for the family and cotton to sell at market. After all that tough work, cotton families through generations have enjoyed curling up in warm home-made quilts at night.

In my cotton travels I gathered boundless images, scents, tastes, emotions, and stories; my journey was a cornucopia of inspiration. In fact, it was a book's worth, thus the birth of *Quilting with Jodie in Cotton Country*. How-to crafting, travelogue, and history, with a bit of humor and a few good recipes mixed in, this is, I think, a new breed of quilting book. Browsing the pages, you are able to share in my adventures and almost see Cotton Country for yourself.

I wish I could complete the experience for you by handing you a Southern treat, such as a delicious, piping-hot fried pie, and letting you wrap your arms around the soft neck of a pinto mule. Instead, as you turn the pages, transport yourself to Cotton Country in your own kitchen, where you can mix up a pitcher of sweet iced tea and wrap your arms around a cozy cotton-boll pillow or a pint-sized mule of your own making. I hope you enjoy the trip through this, my quilt-hug of a book for you. Pass the sweet tea, please!

Jodie Davis

VINTAGE PHOTOS

In a serendipitous moment of good fortune, photographer Rick Stone was introduced to a time capsule of 1,000 vintage glass-plate negatives discovered in an estate sale in his hometown. Taken by amateur photographer and general store owner Cicero Simmons between 1880 and 1925, these photographs document everyday life in a rural Georgia town. Rick Stone painstakingly researched each photo and, using modern high-tech software, digitally developed, preserved, and printed them with special pigments and archival paper. The striking clarity gives the impression that the subjects have walked right out of the past. You will find some of these photos in the pages of *Quilting with Jodie in Cotton Country*. The quality of the photos is a tribute to the skills of both the original photographer and Rick Stone. Contact Vintage Images, 68 AJ Irvin Road, Box 3, Talmo, GA 30575. Tel: (706) 693-4252 or e-mail rickstone@alltel.net.

LIFE *on* *the* FARM

Mules at the plow, wagons bursting with cotton ready for market, children at play, and daisies dancing in the summer breeze—how better to imagine life on a Southern farm? Mix in the delicious tastes and smells from the family farm kitchen and the picture is complete. Hard work in a warm climate generates quite a thirst, which our recipe for the famed southern sweet iced tea stands ready to quench.

THE BOLL WEEVIL SONG

The boll weevil say to the farmer
"You can ride in that Ford machine,
But when I get thru with your cotton
You can't buy gasoline."
Well, the merchant got half
*   the cotton,*
The boll weevils got the rest.
Didn't leave the poor farmer's wife
But one old cotton dress
And it's all full of holes.

—BROOK BENTON AND CLYDE OTIS

C. Billups' Climax Cotton Plow.
Documenting the American South (http://docsouth.unc.edu), The University
of North Carolina at Chapel Hill Libraries, North Carolina Collection

YOU CAN'T BUY GASOLINE." WELL THE MERCHANT GOT HALF THE COTTON, THE BOLL WEEVILS

GOT THE REST, DIDN'T LEAVE THE POOR FARMER'S WIFE BUT ONE OLD COTTON DRESS AND IT'S ALL FULL OF HOLES.

THE BOLL WEEVIL SAY TO THE FARMER "YOU CAN RIDE IN THAT FORD MACHINE, BUT WHEN I GET THRU WITH YOUR COTTON

"THE BOLL WEEVIL SONG"

PEACH JAM

Sunny Southern Sampler

Work by hand or machine to create this charming sampler. The cut-and-fuse appliqué technique helps the quilt come together quickly, and blanket stitch adds a pretty embellishment—as well as hiding any rough edges. Since a separate materials list is provided for each of the ten featured blocks, you can mix and match motifs as you please! As assembled here, the finished quilt measures 48″ × 61″. Fix yourself a pitcher of tea, browse through your fabrics, and sew!

WHO SAYS THERE'S NO MONEY IN COTTON?

That paper dollar in your wallet isn't paper at all. It's a blend of 75 percent cotton lint and 25 percent linen. It takes a 480 pound cotton bale to make 313,600 hundred-dollar bills!

Cabin in the Field
Green background fabric:
  15" × 18"
Brown cabin fabric: 4" × 10"
Brown/gray roof fabric: 3½" × 11"
Brown porch posts, door, and
  window detail fabric: 4" × 7"
Beige window fabric: 3" × 3"
Brick motif fabric for chimney:
  1¼" × 3"
Fusible web: ¾ yard
6-ply embroidery floss to match
  appliqués
7 mm pom-poms for cotton
  bolls in field (available at craft
  stores)

Gloriosa Daisies
Blue background fabric: 13" × 15"
Brown vase fabric: 6" × 6"
Yellow fabrics for flowers, cut 6:
  3½" × 3½" each
Brown daisy centers: Scraps
Green leaves: Scraps
Fusible web: ¾ yard
6-ply embroidery floss to match
  appliqués

See templates A to H on page 97

Cabin in the Field

STEP-BY-STEP

1. Make the appliqué block following the directions on pages 88–89 for fusible appliqué and on page 91 for blanket stitch embroidery. Hand-stitch the pom-pom cotton bolls in the field.

2. Trim the block to 16" × 13½".

See templates A to H on page 98

Gloriosa Daisies

STEP-BY-STEP

1. Make the appliqué block following the directions on pages 88–89 for fusible appliqué and on page 91 for blanket stitch embroidery.

2. Trim the block to 11½" × 13½".

See templates A to C on page 107

Cotton Boll Basket

STEP-BY-STEP

1. Make the appliqués following the directions on pages 88–89 for fusible appliqué. Arrange them and the doily on the background fabric. Trim, turn under, and topstitch the top edge of the doily to the background fabric. Fuse the appliqués in place following the instructions on pages 88–89. Finish with blanket stitch, following the directions on page 91.

2. Trim the block to 11½" × 11½".

See templates on pages 99 to 104

Trio of Mules

STEP-BY-STEP

1. Prepare and apply the appliqués following the directions on pages 88–89. Since some portions overlap the borders, you will need to complete the appliqués once the borders are in place.

2. Cut the green/brown fabric for the border into 4½"-wide strips. For the side borders cut two pieces, each 12" long. For the top and bottom borders, cut two pieces, each 27" long.

3. Stitch the shorter pieces to the sides of the block. Press the seam allowances toward the border pieces. Stitch the long pieces to the top and bottom of the block. Press the seam allowances toward the border pieces.

4. Complete the fusing of all appliqué pieces. Blanket stitch around the appliqués following the directions on page 91.

5. Trim the block to 27" × 20½", if necessary.

MATERIALS LIST

Cotton Boll Basket
Beige background fabric:
   13" × 14"
Doily: 9" wide or smaller
Brown fabric for basket: 8" × 8"
White fabric for cotton bolls:
   3" × 15"
Brown fabric for cotton boll
   stems: 3" × 15"
Fusible web: ½ yard
6-ply embroidery floss to match
   appliqués

Trio of Mules
Gold background fabric:
   19" × 12½"
Green/brown fabric for border:
   ⅜ yard
Fusible web: 3 yards
6-ply embroidery floss to match
   appliqués

BROWN MULE (left)
Brown fabric for head and ears:
   10" × 13"
Beige fabric for nose: 4" × 4"
Dark brown fabric for outside
   collar: 5½" × 7½"
Light brown fabric for inside
   collar: 4" × 7½"
Beige/gold fabric for collar knob:
   2" × 2"
Contrasting brown fabric for
   inner ear: 4" × 4"
Beige and brown fabric for eyes
   and nostrils: 3" × 3"

GRAY MULE (middle)
Gray fabric for head and ears:
   15" × 14"
Gray print for nose: 4" × 4"
Light gray fabric for eyelids:
   2" × 2"
Black fabric for eyes and nostrils:
   3" × 3"

GOLD MULE (right)
Gold fabric for head and ears:
   8" × 14"
Bright gold fabric for hat: 5" × 8"
Contrast fabric for inner ears,
   eyes, nose, and mouth: 5" × 5"
Yellow fabric for flowers, cut 2:
   4" × 4" each
Green fabric for flower leaf and
   stem: 2" × 3"
Brown fabric for daisy centers:
   scraps

MATERIALS LIST

Cotton Wagons
Blue background fabric: 13″ × 25″
White tone-on-tone print for
    cotton: 8″ × 6″ piece plus
    6″ × 2½″ piece
Brown fabric for wagon sides:
    7½″ × 6″
Brown fabric for wagon wheels:
    7″ × 11″
Fusible web: ½ yard
6-ply embroidery floss to match
    appliqués

Pot of Geraniums
Yellow background fabric:
    12½″ × 14″
Gray fabric for pot: 5″ × 6″
Red fabric for geraniums: 4″ × 8″
Green fabric for leaves: 4″ × 11″
Fusible web: ½ yard
6-ply embroidery floss to match
    appliqués
Small beads to embellish
    geraniums (optional)

See templates A to C on pages 108–109

Cotton Wagons

STEP-BY-STEP

1. Cut the brown fabric for the wagon sides into 12 strips measuring 7½″ × ½″.

2. Position template A first, then place B on top of it. Fuse both pieces. Trim as necessary to make the two pieces align nicely. Fuse the strips from step 1 on top of A/B to form the wagon sides. Continue to make the appliqué block following the directions on pages 88–89 for fusible appliqué and on page 91 for blanket stitch embroidery.

3. Trim the block to 11½″ × 22½″.

See templates A to C on page 112

Pot of Geraniums

STEP-BY-STEP

1. Make the appliqué block following the directions on pages 88–89 for fusible appliqué and on page 91 for blanket stitch embroidery. Hand-stitch the beads randomly to the geraniums.

2. Trim the block to 12″ × 11½″.

Unloading cotton bales at the dock.

Reproduced by permission of Rick Stone.

Murphy Cotton Gin in Talmo, Jackson County, Georgia, c. 1900.

See templates A to E on pages 110–111

Farm Kids

STEP-BY-STEP

1. Make the appliqué block following the directions on pages 88–89 for fusible appliqué and on page 91 for blanket stitch embroidery. Hand sew the buttons to the dresses and overalls.

2. Trim the block to $42\frac{1}{2}'' \times 11\frac{1}{2}''$.

MATERIALS LIST

Farm Kids
Green background fabric:
    14" × 44"
Doll bodies, cut 5: 10"x 10" each
Doll dresses, cut 3: 5" × 6" each
Doll overalls, cut 2: 5" × 7" each
Girl's hair, cut 3: 4" × 4" each
Boy's hat, cut 2: 3" × 5" each
Pocket and patch: red scraps
Fusible web: ¾ yard
6-ply embroidery floss to match
    appliqués
Buttons

COTTON TIMELINE

3000 BC

Cotton is grown in India

1300

Cliff dwellers in New Mexico grow cotton

1607

The first cotton crops are planted in South Carolina

1787

The first cotton mill is opened in Massachusetts

1790

The first successful crop of Sea Island cotton is raised on Hilton Head Island, South Carolina

Samuel Slater erects a water-powered cotton yarn mill in Rhode Island

1793

Eli Whitney invents the cotton gin

1806

Mexican hybrid cotton is intro-duced into the US

1845

Cotton button-fly pants are the latest fashion statement, despite protests from the religious community, who see the flap as a license to sin

1890

The mule-drawn cotton picker is patented

1892

Boll weevils enter the US from Mexico

1903

Cotton covers the wings of the Wright brothers' airplane

An Up-Country cotton press.

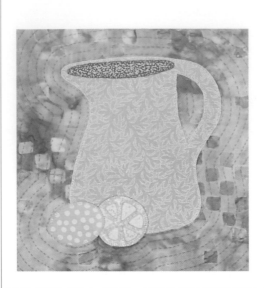

MATERIALS LIST

Sweet Iced Tea
Green background fabric:
    13″ × 14″
Beige fabric for pitcher: 8″ × 9″
Red-brown fabric for iced tea:
    2″ × 6″
Yellow fabric for lemons,
    cut 3 from assorted yellows:
    3″ × 3″ each
Fusible web: ½ yard
6-ply embroidery floss to match
    appliqués

Bowl of Peaches
Light beige background fabric:
    13″ × 14″
Blue bowl fabric: 5″ × 9″
Dark blue fabric for bowl rim:
    2″ × 9″
Peaches, cut 9 from assorted
    fabrics: 3″ × 3″ each
Green leaves, cut 6 from assorted
    fabrics: 2½″ × 4″ each
Peach pit: brown scrap
Fusible web: ¾ yard
6-ply embroidery floss to match
    appliqués

See templates A to E on page 113

Sweet Iced Tea

STEP-BY-STEP

1. Make the appliqué block following the directions on pages 88–89 for fusible appliqué and on page 91 for blanket stitch embroidery.

2. Trim the block to 10½″ × 11½″.

See templates A to F on page 114

Bowl of Peaches

STEP-BY-STEP

1. Make the appliqué block following the directions on pages 88–89 for fusible appliqué and on page 91 for blanket stitch embroidery.

2. Trim the block to 12″ × 11½″.

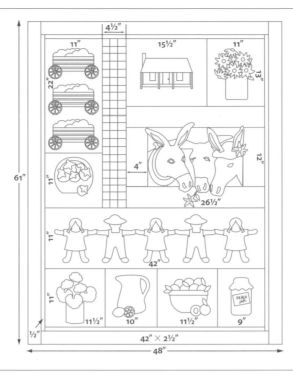

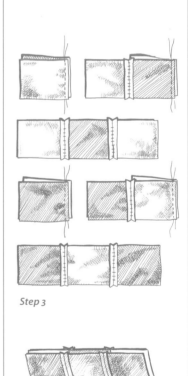

See templates A to C on page 115

Peach Jam

STEP-BY-STEP

1. Make the appliqué block following the directions on pages 88–89 for fusible appliqué and on page 91 for blanket stitch embroidery. Transfer the markings, then stitch the jar label with a running stitch following the directions on page 91. Before fusing the green jar lid, insert the ends of the string behind the appliqué and tie together.

2. Trim the block to 9½″ × 11½″.

All seam allowances are ¼″ unless specified otherwise.

Full-Quilt Assembly

STEP-BY-STEP

1. Turn to pages 4 to 11 to complete all ten blocks.

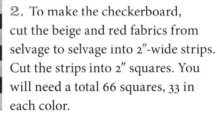

Checkerboard

2. To make the checkerboard, cut the beige and red fabrics from selvage to selvage into 2″-wide strips. Cut the strips into 2″ squares. You will need a total 66 squares, 33 in each color.

3. Stitch the squares into strips of three, alternating colors as shown. Press the seam allowances to one side. Stitch rows together to form the checkerboard (see also directions for chain piecing on pages 87–88). Press.

Block assembly

4. Arrange the blocks and the inner checkerboard as in the photograph. Stitch the blocks together in the following order, then press well:

- Stitch Cabin to Gloriosa Daisies
- Stitch Mules to Cabin/Gloriosa Daisies
- Stitch Checkerboard to left-hand side of Mules/Cabin/Gloriosa Daisies

MATERIALS LIST

Peach Jam
Blue background fabric: 11″ × 13″
Peach fabric for jam jar: 5″ × 8″
Light beige fabric for label: 3″ × 4″
Green fabric for jam jar lid: 3″ × 6″
Fusible web: ¼ yard
6-ply embroidery floss to match appliqués
Soft string: 12″ or less

Full-Quilt Assembly
Checkerboard strip: ⅛ yard each of beige and red fabrics
Inner border: ¼ yard brown fabric
Outer border: ½ yard cream fabric
Binding: ½ yard green fabric
Backing fabric: 54″ × 67″
Batting: 54″ x 67″
6-ply embroidery floss to match appliqués

Step 3

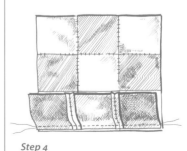

Step 4

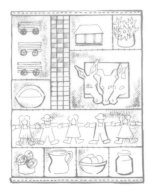

Step 5

Step 6

Step 8

Farmer plowing with mule in cotton field, Jackson County, Georgia c. 1900.

Reproduced by permission of Rick Stone.

- Stitch Cotton Basket to bottom of Cotton Boll Wagons
- Stitch Cotton Boll Wagons/Cotton Basket to right-hand side of Checkerboard
- Stitch Farm Kids to resulting bottom edge
- Stitch Geraniums to Iced Tea and Peaches to Peach Jam
- Stitch Geraniums/Iced Tea to Peaches/Peach Jam
- Stitch to bottom of Farm Kids

Inner border

5. Cut the brown fabric selvage to selvage into five 1″ strips. Measure the quilt top horizontally, from side to side, across the center. Cut two of the brown strips this length. Stitch to the top and bottom of the quilt top.

6. Measure the quilt top vertically, from top to bottom, across the center. Piece the remaining strips to obtain this length. Stitch to either side of the quilt top. Press the seam allowances toward the brown strips.

Outer border

7. Cut and piece the cream fabric into two strips measuring 3″ × 42½″ and two strips measuring approximately 3″ × 60½″. (To be absolutely accurate, measure the width and length of your quilt top across the center to determine the correct length of the strips to cut.) Transfer the Boll Weevil song, as in the photograph on page 2, onto the outer border strips. You can either write freehand on the fabric using a light marker, or choose a computer font to type, print, then trace the words onto the fabric. Embroider each letter with running stitch (see page 91).

8. Stitch the top and bottom strips to the quilt. Press the seam allowances. Stitch the remaining strips in place along the sides of the quilt top. Press the seam allowances.

Finishing

9. Turn to pages 92–94 for directions on sandwiching, quilting, and binding your quilt. Add a hanging sleeve as directed on page 95. Don't forget the label!

Mule Wallhanging

SMITTEN WITH THE MULES I saw during my Southern travels, I found images of those docile creatures would crop up in my mind whenever I sat down at my design table. Their sweet, patient nature, kind eyes, Roman noses, and those long ears lend themselves so well to soft crafts.

Using the templates from Sunny Southern Sampler on page 2 (see templates on pages 99–104), I couldn't resist putting together this simple wall hanging. I distinguished my Molly—or female mule—from the two Johns with a sunflower and hat. The finished size is just 28″ × 23″. Begin with a green background square measuring 17½″ × 11½″, and modify the templates and colors as you please to come up with a trio of mules all your own. Construct the block in exactly the same way as you made the blocks of my Sunny Southern Sampler, using the same fusing technique. If you want your design to overlap the borders like mine, simply hold off on fusing the blue overlapping sections until the green border is added. You will need about 3 yards of fusible web, a 32″ × 26″ piece of batting, plus the same size rectangle of backing fabric. You'll also need about ½ yard of fabric for outer border, binding, and hanging sleeve.

STUBBORN AS A MULE?

So, what exactly *is* a mule? It's the hybrid offspring of a donkey stallion and a horse mare. It was George Washington who, in 1785, first imported donkey stallions into the United States and bred them to mares to produce mules for the U.S. Army. Mules have been pegged with a reputation for stubbornness and even laziness, but nothing, as any mule-lover will tell you, could be further from the truth. The fact is that mules have a keen sense of danger and will not willingly put themselves in its way. By refusing to budge, a mule is simply trying to report that things aren't right. Sounds smart to me!

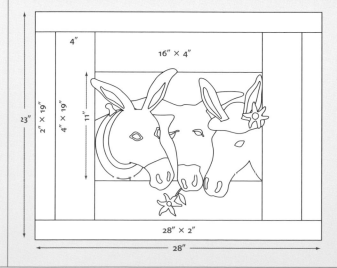

Add texture and dimension with turn-and-stuff appliqué.

Cotton Basket Pillow

MATERIALS LIST
Background (tabletop):
    3½″ × 10½″
Background (wallpaper):
    7½″ × 10½″
9″ or smaller doily
Brown basket fabric: 8″ × 16″
White cotton boll fabric: 9″ × 14″
Brown cotton boll stem fabric:
    6″ × 14″
Red border strips, cut 4:
    ½″ × 10½″
Brown outer border strips, cut 4:
    4½″ × 10½″
Pillow back, cut 2: 12½″ × 18½″
Scraps of batting and fiberfill to
    stuff cotton and basket
18″ square pillow form

Fresh-from-the-fields cotton bolls are a pretty sight, and what better way to display them than in a basket? To give the cotton appliqués extra dimension, I used a two-layer turn-and-stuff method. This is a great project for digging through your fabric scraps stash. The appliqué sizes are approximate, so you can choose any scraps that work well on your pillow.

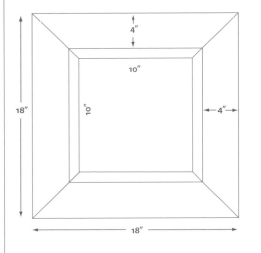

See templates A to C on page 107. All seam allowances are ¼" unless specified otherwise

Cotton Basket Pillow

STEP-BY-STEP

1. Place the "tabletop" background fabric right side up on the sewing surface, the long edge horizontal. Lay the doily wrong side down on the right side of the fabric. Decide how much of the doily you wish to show. Trim even with the cut edge of the fabric. This will be the top edge of the table. Lay the "wallpaper" background fabric on top of the doily, right side down. Stitch the three layers together.

2. Press the red inner-border strips in half lenthwise. Place one strip along a side edge of the background. Baste. Repeat for the second side, then the top and bottom edges.

3. Center a brown border strip on one edge, right side facing the right side of the background fabric. Stitch, starting and ending ¼" from the corner of the background square, backstitching at each end, and catching the red inner border in the stitching. Repeat for the three remaining sides.

4. To miter the corners, right sides facing, match adjacent border strips. Using a 45° angle, mark a stitching line on one border strip by lining the angle up with the raw edge of the border strip and the end of the stitching. Stitch. Trim the seam allowances to ¼" and press.

❝ JODIE SAYS

To make your pillow soft to the touch, try making the cotton bolls from a textured fabric, such as velvet or velour scraps. ❞

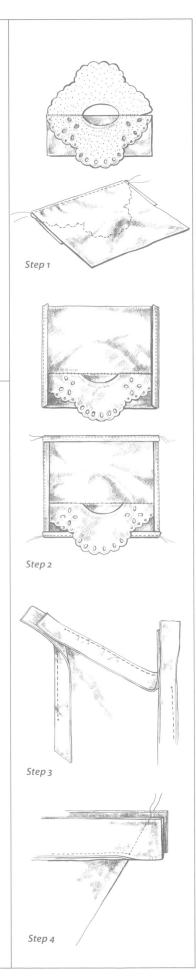

Step 1

Step 2

Step 3

Step 4

Sweet Tea

SWEET ICED TEA

Makes two quarts

2-quart or 8-cup size tea bags—
  Luzianne brand is a popular choice
  in the South!
8 cups boiling water
2 cups fresh mint
½ cup to 1 cup sugar

Combine all of the ingredients and let steep for 20 minutes. Strain, chill, and serve over ice.

If this is not sweet enough for you, transform it into Lemonade Sweet Tea by mixing one part sweet tea with one part lemonade.

ORANGE CRANBERRY TEA

Makes one quart

1 cup orange juice
1 cup cranberry juice
2 tbsp sugar
1 cinnamon stick
4 tea bags
2 cups water

In a medium saucepan, stir together the orange juice, cranberry juice, sugar and water. Add a cinnamon stick and bring to the boil. Reduce the heat, then cover and simmer for ten minutes. Remove from the heat and add the tea bags. Cover and let stand for five minutes. Remove and discard the tea bags and cinnamon stick. Chill. Serve over ice and garnish with orange slices.

SWEET "TAY" or sweet tea flows the whole year round in the South. And when they say "sweet" they mean it! The oldest sweet tea recipe in print comes from Marion Cabell Tyree's Housekeeping in Old Virginia, published in 1879. Mrs. Tyree let fresh green tea leaves steep in water all day. She would then add first ice, next sugar, then a squeeze of lemon. The first recipe using black tea, which became the convention, dates back to 1884.

The 1904 World's Fair, held in St. Louis in celebration of the Louisiana Purchase, popularized and commercialized iced tea. One very hot summer day, a group of Indian tea producers found that passers-by ignored their wares. Desperate to sell the tea, Richard Blechynden, an Englishman directing the tea pavilion, packed ice cubes into glasses and poured tea over it. Word spread and thirsty fair-goers lined up to buy the cool beverage.

On any given day, approximately half of the American population drinks tea, with the greatest concentrations in the South and Northeast. Southerners have come to see the comedy in their keenness for sweet iced tea. On a recent April Fool's Day, a State Representative from Georgia introduced House Bill 819, proposing that all Georgia restaurants be required to serve sweet tea!

Ad Davis checks the grade and quality of two 500 pound bales of cotton in front of a local store in Talmo, Georgia c. 1900.

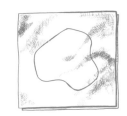

Step 5

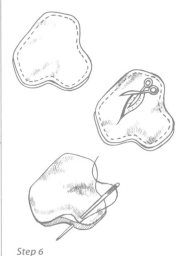

Step 6

5. Trace all the appliqué pattern pieces onto their respective fabrics, following the directions on the pattern pieces. Place the traced fabric onto another piece of fabric, right sides facing. Cut each piece out, leaving roughly ½″ of fabric around each shape. For the basket handle, basket body, and cotton boll stems, place the two layers on top of a piece of batting, stitching lines facing up.

6. For all but the basket handle, stitch along the drawn lines, overlapping the stitching at beginning and end. Leave the two ends of the handle unstitched. Cut each appliqué piece out, leaving about ⅛″ of seam allowance. Turn the basket handle right sides out. For all of the other appliqués, make a slit through one fabric thickness and turn the shapes

right sides out. Stuff the cotton bolls with fiberfill and stitch the opening closed.

7. Arrange the appliqués on the pillow background, placing the basket handle under the basket and arranging the cotton bolls as you wish. Tack them down.

8. Press under 1″ along one longer edge of each pillow back. Turn under ¼″. Topstitch.

9. Right sides facing the pillow top, lay one pillow backing over the other, raw edges matching the outside edges of the pillow top, and the finished edges of the pillow backs overlapping. Stitch all the way around the outside edges of the pillow, overlapping the beginning and end stitching. Turn right side out and insert pillow form.

Step 7

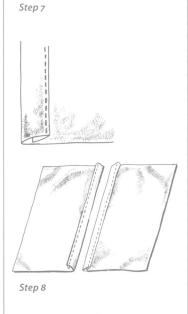

Step 8

Right and below: Cotton bales and cotton plants in the field.

Frogmore Plantation

Cotton on the gin.

A DAY AT FROGMORE PLANTATION is a window into the story of cotton in the South. Dating from the early 19th century, this 1,800-acre farm has witnessed two hundred years of Southern history, with all its joys and sorrows. Today, Frogmore, a modern working cotton farm and gin, embraces the present while preserving the past. Owners George "Buddy" and Lynette Tanner reside in the original 1815 raised-basement planters' house, listed on the National Register of Historic Buildings. To recreate a typical Southern plantation, the Tanners have collected centuries-old farm buildings from an 80-mile radius. After researching extensive archives and accumulating oral histories, Buddy and Lynette sought to provide an accurate living history experience for visitors who, in a two-hour tour, journey back through Southern history.

This unique interpretive tour begins with clomping up steps onto the wide wood plank porch of the Frogmore General Store. As I made my way through the squeaky screened door into the vintage mercantile, my senses began to soak in the essence of a bygone era. I felt I had stepped back in time. The fact that my guide—the daughter of a former sharecropper who worked the plantation—was dressed in period costume enhanced the illusion. Together, we examined the smokehouse, a log cabin barn, the wash house, the pigeon roost, a dogtrot, and even a three-hole privy! I was overwhelmed to think of the sheer amount of work it took to provide the necessities of life on a self-sufficient plantation.

Quieted by the slow pace of the days gone by, we passed fields of cotton gleaming white in the sun and surfaced in the 21st century at the Tanner gin. Decidedly modern-day trucks deliver mammoth 20,000-pound rectangular loads of harvested cotton for ginning and subsequent baling; then it's off to manufacturing facilities far and wide. Inside the gin I was again surprised at the juxtaposition of old and new. Technology has made cotton ginning more an enterprise of bytes than brawn. The roar of the gin, the screech of truck brakes, and the smell of diesel fuel are signs of a modern level of efficiency that enables today's cotton ginning families to make a living while serving our timeless need for and love of cotton.

I drove away from Frogmore Plantation aware of its difficult history but filled with admiration for the ingenuity and the pure grit of our forefathers and mothers. Lynette and Buddy are modern-day equivalents of the hardy farmers who have raised cotton at Frogmore for two hundred years. We quilters and fabric lovers thank you!

KITCHEN CAPERS

Family life on Southern farms was a simple one, well-versed in making do. For what they lacked in fancy worldly goods, Southern farming families made up in the kitchen. The tradition holds true today—the kitchen is the center of family and social life.

Southerners use their ingenuity to fry just about anything. Fried chicken and catfish are staples, fried apple pies delightful, and fried okra and green tomatoes count as vegetable servings. And don't forget the can of shortening to make the fluffy biscuits that accompany almost every meal.

Cut-and-fuse appliqué, trimmed with blanket stitch, with quick, pieced-squares border.

SOUTHERN HOSPITALITY

Farm life followed Mother Nature's ages-old seasonal to-do list, with food preservation taking center stage every fall. This meant canning farm-grown fruits and vegetables into glass jars and lining them up on pantry shelves to satisfy hungry tummies all winter long. For Southern families, local peaches and corn typically filled those jars, a colorful display of the delicious tastes of summer inside. See the recipe for *Pickled Peaches,* opposite and for *Corn Relish* on page 28.

Pantry Pictures Wall Hanging

Bright and cheery, this quilted hanging will bring back warm memories of Southern hospitality and the delicious fruits and preserves of Cotton Country. The wall hanging comes together quickly by machine and even by hand—picture yourself on a sunny Southern porch as you stitch away! The flowers, fruits, and bowls are all cut-and-fuse appliqué, trimmed with blanket stitch. The outer border is pieced from brightly colored squares, and the entire quilt is finished with simple diagonal quilting lines. This picture-window into Southern living measures just 27½″ × 30″, and will fit into a favorite nook or cranny in your own kitchen.

PICKLED PEACHES
Makes six 1-pint jars

Make up a batch of this Southern specialty to serve with chicken, ham, or barbequed pork.

4 lbs. peaches
4 cups granulated sugar
2 cups white vinegar
1 cup water
3 cinnamon sticks, 3″ long, broken
1 tbsp whole cloves
1/2 tsp whole allspice
1 tsp lemon juice
6 pint jars with 2-piece lids

1. Bring a saucepan of water to a rolling boil. Dip the peaches for about 30 seconds and slip off the skins. Place in an ice water solution of 8 cups water and 1 tsp lemon juice.

2. In a large non-reactive saucepan, bring sugar, vinegar, and water to a boil, stirring until the sugar is dissolved. Tie cinnamon, cloves, and allspice in a cheesecloth bag and add to the syrup. Reduce the heat and boil gently for 15 minutes.

3. Drain the peaches and add them to the syrup. Return to a boil and boil gently for 5 minutes. Discard spice bag.

4. Remove the peaches from the liquid with a slotted spoon and pack them into sterilized hot pint jars. Ladle syrup to within ½″ of the rim, covering peaches. Wipe the rims and seal. Process in a boiling water bath or canner for 20 minutes (for pint jars).

5. Remove the jars from the canner and complete the seals.

NOTE: Any large cooking pot with a tight-fitting lid can be used as a canner, and a round cake rack can be substituted for the canner rack. Place the filled jars on the rack of a canner containing boiling water. Adjust the water level to cover the jars by about an inch. Cover the canner and return the water to a boil. Start counting the processing time when the water has returned to a steady boil.

MATERIALS

Pot of Geraniums
Dark green background print:
  11½″ × 13″
Brown fabric for pot: 5″ × 6″
Red fabric for geraniums: 4″ × 9″
Green fabric for leaves: 4″ × 11″
Fusible web: ¼ yard
6-ply embroidery floss to match
  appliqués
Small red beads to embellish
  geraniums (optional)

Gloriosa Daisy
Light orange background print:
  11½″ × 13″
Brown fabric for vase: 6″ × 6″
Flowers, cut 6 assorted yellow
  fabrics: 3½″ × 3½″ each
Brown daisy centers: Scraps
Green leaves: Scraps
Fusible web: ¼ yard
6-ply embroidery floss to match
  appliqués

See templates A to C on page 112

Pot of Geraniums

STEP-BY-STEP

1. Working on the pot first, followed by the leaves, then the flowers, make the appliqué block following the directions on pages 88–89 for fusible appliqué and on page 91 for blanket stitch embroidery.

2. Trim the block to 11″ × 12¼″.

See templates A to H on page 98

Gloriosa Daisy

STEP-BY-STEP

1. Working on the vase first, followed by the leaves, then the flowers, make the appliqué block following the directions on pages 88–89 for fusible appliqué and on page 91 for blanket stitch embroidery.

2. Trim the block to 11″ × 12¼″.

See templates A to E on page 113. Reverse templates A and E

Iced Tea

STEP-BY-STEP

1. Working on the pitcher first, then the lemons, make the appliqué block following the directions on pages 88–89 for fusible appliqué and on page 91 for blanket stitch embroidery.

2. Trim the block to 11″ × 12¼″.

See templates A to F on page 114

Bowl of Peaches

STEP-BY-STEP

1. Working on the peaches inside the bowl first, then the bowl, then the remaining peaches and leaves, make the appliqué block following the directions on pages 88–89 for fusible appliqué and on page 91 for blanket stitch embroidery.

2. Trim the block to 11″ × 12¼″.

MATERIALS

Iced Tea
Light orange background print:
    11½″ × 13″
Blue fabric for pitcher: 8″ × 9″
Dark blue print for inside of
    pitcher: 2″ × 6″
Pale yellow fabric for lemon, cut
    2: 3″ × 3″ each
Bright yellow fabric for inside of
    lemon: 3″ × 3″
Fusible web: ¼ yard
6-ply embroidery floss to match
    appliqués

Bowl of Peaches
Dark green background print:
    11½″ × 13″
Blue fabric for bowl: 5″ × 9″
Dark blue print for bowl rim:
    2″ × 9″
Red, pink, and orange fabrics for
    peaches, cut 9: 3″ × 3″ each
Green leaves, cut 6: Scraps
Peach pit: brown scrap
Fusible web: ¼ yard
6-ply embroidery floss to match
    appliqués

MATERIALS

Full Quilt Assembly
Inner border: ⅜ yard blue fabric
Outer border: 42 3″ × 3″ squares
  from assorted fabrics
Backing: 33″ × 36″
Batting: 33″ × 36″
Binding: ¼ yard forest green
  fabric

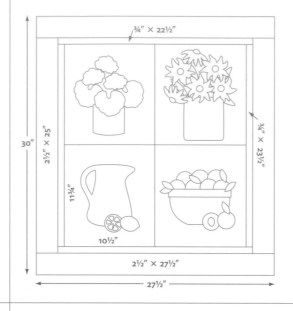

All seam allowances are ¼″ unless specified otherwise

Full-Quilt Assembly

STEP-BY-STEP

1. Turn to pages 24–25 to complete all four blocks. Stitch together, as shown.

2. Cut the blue inner-border fabric into 1¼″-wide strips, selvage to selvage. From these strips, cut two side-border pieces measuring 24″ long, Cut the top and bottom inner-border pieces at 23″ long.

3. Stitch the two longer blue inner-border strips to the sides of the quilt. Press the seam allowances to one side. Stitch the remaining blue inner-border strips to the top and bottom edges of the quilt. Press the seam allowances to one side.

❜ JODIE SAYS

Notice that the wall hanging is made with the same motifs and templates used in *Sunny Southern Sampler* on page 2. Use any of those motifs in your wall hanging and modify or embellish as you please. ❞

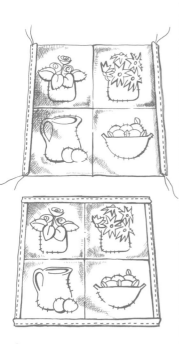

Step 1

Step 3

A southern plow team.

4. Stitch the 3″ squares randomly into four sets: two sets of ten squares each for the side borders, and two of eleven squares each for the top and bottom borders. Sew the rows of ten squares to the sides of the quilts. Press the seam allowances to one side. Sew the remaining two strips of eleven squares to the top and bottom of the quilt. Press the seam allowances to one side.

5. Turn to page 92 for directions on assembling the quilt layers in preparation for quilting. Quilt around the appliquéd images, in diagonal rows 1″ apart in the block backgrounds, and diagonally across the border squares.

6. Follow the directions on pages 93–94 to bind your quilt and on page 95 to add a hanging sleeve.

Step 4

CORN RELISH

Makes six to seven 1-pint jars

In jars packed with summer sunshine, this sweet and sour relish is a healthy addition to hot dogs, and it looks pretty to boot!

20 ears sweet corn (2½ quarts kernels or 10 cups frozen, defrosted)
1 cup chopped green pepper
1 cup chopped sweet red pepper
1½ cups chopped onion
1 cup chopped celery
2 cups sugar
2 tbsp mustard seeds
1 tbsp salt
1½ tsp celery seeds
½ tsp ground turmeric
3¼ cups cider vinegar
2 cups water
7 pint jars with 2-piece lids

1. If using fresh corn, boil for 5 minutes. Plunge the cobs into cold water. Cut the kernels from the cobs and measure about 10 cups.

2. Combine all ingredients and simmer for 20 minutes.

3. Pack into clean, hot sterilized pint jars, leaving 1" head space. Make certain the vinegar solution covers the vegetables. Wipe the rims and seal.

4. Adjust lids and process in boiling water bath (212°F) for 20 minutes. See note on canning on page 23.

5. Remove the jars from the canner and complete the seals. The flavor will develop over several days.

Gloriosa Daisy Apron

What's one of today's hottest collectibles? Vintage aprons! Ranging from traditional neck-to-hem utilitarian cover-ups to 1930s styles made from brightly printed feedsack cloth to the frilliest party aprons, there have been times when no self-respecting Southern farm cook would venture into her kitchen without one.

This easy-to-sew apron is made up of fabric squares and rectangles—no pattern required. It's a cinch to modify the size to fit, and you can decorate it with whatever appliqué motifs you please. Add the Gloriosa Daisy appliqué to bring summer into your kitchen all year round.

MATERIALS

42"-wide denim: 1¼ yards
Flower appliqué: Scraps of
   yellow, brown and green
Spool of matching thread
Two 1" D rings
Fusible web: ⅛ yard

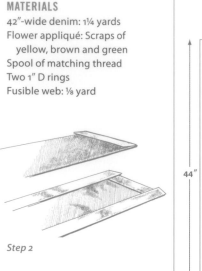

Step 2

Step 3

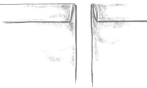

Step 4

Step 5

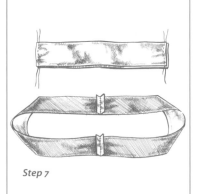

Step 7

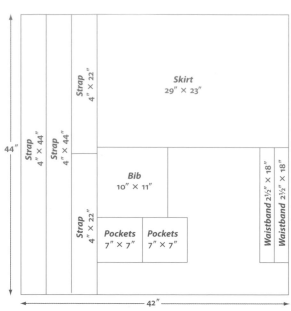

Gloriosa Daisy Apron

STEP-BY-STEP

1. Cut the following pieces:
   Two straps: 4" × 44"
   Two straps: 4" × 22"
   One bib: 10" × 11"
   One skirt: 29" × 23"
   Two pockets: 7" × 7"
   Two waistbands: 2½" × 18"

2. Piece each short strap end to end to a long strap. Fold up ½" on one short end of each strap and press. Fold a ½" hem on each long side and press.

3. Fold the straps in half lengthwise and press.

4. Along one of the 10" sides of the bib, fold a ¼" hem, fold another ¼" (making a double hem) and stitch.

5. To attach the straps to the 11" sides of the bib, pin the unfinished end of the strap to the side edge of the bib, enclosing ½" of the bib in the seam. Stitch to the bib and continue stitching the strap to the end. Repeat for the second strap.

6. To hem the skirt, fold and press a double hem (see Step 4) on one long side and two short sides of the skirt. Stitch the hems.

7. Stitch the ends of the two waistband pieces together into a loop using a ½" seam allowance. Press seams open.

Dickerson family picking cotton c. 1910.

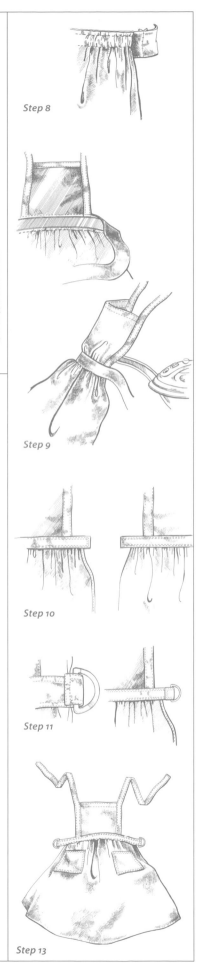

Step 8

Step 9

Step 10

Step 11

Step 13

8. Gather the top edge of the skirt with two rows of basting stitches, one just less than ½″ from the raw edge, and another about ¼″ from the raw edge. Pull on the threads to gather the skirt to 16.″ Pin the skirt to the waistband beginning 1″ from a seam and ending 1″ before the second seam. Stitch with a ½″ seam allowance.

9. Attach the bib to the waistband, centering over the skirt. Stitch with a ½″ seam allowance. Press a ½″ hem on all loose sides of the waistband.

10. Form the facing by folding at the end seams and top stitch together enclosing the seams for the bib and skirt.

11. Attach the D rings by folding the ends of the waistband back ½″ and top stitching securely.

12. For the pockets, press under ¼″, then ¾″ on one side and stitch. This is the top of the pocket. Press a double ¼″ hem on the other sides and stitch.

13. Follow the directions on pages 88–89 to prepare the fusible appliqués and fuse them in place (see also templates A to H on page 98). Blanket stitch their edges by hand or machine, as instructed on page 91. Place the pockets in a pleasing position on the skirt front and topstitch in place.

Country Rag Rug

The kitchen door is always open in Cotton Country. Friends and neighbors will drop in at any time for a wedge of peach pie and a generous dollop of conversation. So invite them to wipe off their work boots and walk right in!

Anything goes for this project—nothing has to match—as each nine-patch block stands on its own. Use one dark and one light fabric in each block. Just remember when you start stitching a new block that a light color touches a dark color, so that half your blocks will have five lights and four darks; the other half will have four lights and five darks. The rug shown here is 28″ × 22″, but you can easily make it larger simply by adding more blocks.

MATERIALS

36″ wide latch-hook canvas (3¾ holes to the inch): 1 yard

Assorted light fabrics: Twelve ¼ yard pieces or fat quarters

Assorted dark fabrics: Twelve ¼ yard pieces or fat quarters

Dark fabric for outside border: 1½ yards

Rug binding: 3 yards

Sewing thread to match border rows

Size #13 tapestry needle (this is about as large as it gets!)

Masking tape

Carpet binding

Heavy duty staple gun

Plywood board, larger than rug canvas

Step 2

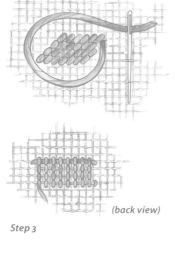

(back view)

Step 3

Country Rag Rug

STEP-BY-STEP

1. To prevent it from raveling, wrap all the raw edges of the canvas with the masking tape.

2. It's easier to cut the strips you'll need one nine-patch block at a time. Cut the strips 1¼″ wide, cutting across the selvage-to-selvage width. If using selvage-to-selvage quarter yards, cut the lengths in half so your "yarn" will not be too long. If you're using fat quarters, the length will be fine. Fold then press these strips in half, lengthwise, wrong sides together.

3. Start your first block at the upper right edge of the canvas, about 4″ in from the top and side (to allow room for the border, to be added later). Stitch one complete "patch" of the nine patch at a time. To begin, bring the "yarn" up from the back of the canvas to the front, leaving 1″ of yarn on the back side. Work with stab stitches, weaving in and out of the canvas. Pull the yarn into position, but don't pull too tight as this may distort your canvas. As you stitch the first row, the yarn will be held in place by your stitches. For each square, stitch eight stitches across, eight rows tall. When the yarn gets too short to work, slide the needle under a few worked stitches on the back side, pull the yarn tight, and cut off leaving a 1″ tail.

4. When all the blocks are completed, stitch five rows of the darker fabric yarn around the entire design as a border.

5. Stitching may cause a degree of distortion in your canvas. Blocking will take care of this. Use a permanent marker to mark the dimensions of the finished rug on the plywood. Staple the rug at even intervals through the unfinished canvas, beginning with the corners. Dampen the rug well with a spray bottle and allow to dry.

6. Trim the excess canvas to 1½″ all around. Turn it under the border and stitch down at the back. Sew carpet binding over the raw edges, mitering the corners.

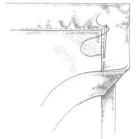

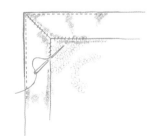

Step 6

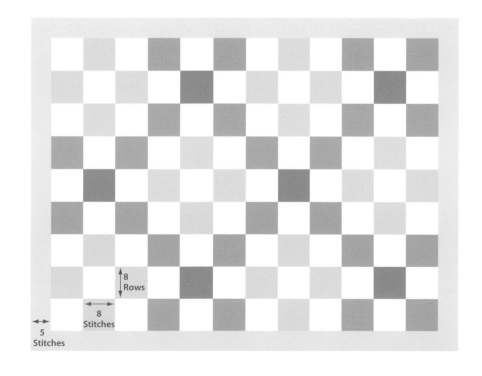

THAT INCREDIBLE MACHINE
The Cotton Gin

Cotton being graded and labeled before loaded on a train and shipped to the cotton mill c. 1900.

DID YOU KNOW that before Eli Whitney's famed cotton gin, the major commodities produced in the South were rice and tobacco? It's easy to see why—it took a full day to produce a single pound of cotton by separating the seeds from the fiber by hand! The new cotton gin cleaned fifty pounds of cotton a day—and Southern plantations quickly rose to the challenge of filling the insatiable hunger of English textile factories for American cotton. With the help of this miraculous invention, cotton production increased from a meager one-hundred and eighty thousand pounds in 1793 to over six million pounds in 1795. By 1810, an astonishing ninety-three million pounds were delivered to gins each year.

Of course, the cotton gin influenced our history in less benevolent ways, too. To supply the growing demands of mill owners in England and New England, planters needed workers in the cotton fields. It was not until 1808 that Congress put a halt to the importation of slaves.

The average yield of cotton today is twice that of the early Colonists. Due to plant genetics and the use of modern fertilizers, cotton growers are able to produce one bale per acre. Some of the seed left over from producing cotton lint is saved for replanting. The remainder is sold to make such products as linoleum, putty, cattle feed, fertilizer, and cooking oil. Even the *linters*, the fuzz that clings to the seed after ginning, provides cellulose to make plastics, X-ray films, and padding for mattresses and furniture.

Murphy Cotton Gin—Talmo, Jackson County, Georgia c. 1900.

There is as much
dignity in plowing
a field as there is in
writing a poem.

BOOKER T. WASHINGTON

BOUNTY *from* *the* COTTON FIELD

Holding in my hand a dry brown boll, bursting with fluffy white cotton, it is amazing to contemplate the lengthy transformation it undergoes before evolving into fabric. Each cotton boll, filled with seeds (and there are a lot of them in a single boll), takes from 45 to 60 days to mature and produces about 50,000 cotton fibers, each measuring about 1⅛″ to 1¾″. Just imagine how many bolls it takes to make a yard of beautiful quilting fabric!

Just Peachy Picnic Quilt

It's summer . . . and time for a picnic! Head for the nearest meadow and lie back on this peachy quilt for a lazy afternoon of sunshine. Or spread the quilt in front of the fire for an indoor picnic, bringing summer sun to the dreariest winter day. Few quilt patterns are easier than a simple nine-patch, and the jiffy stenciling technique used here for the succulent peaches means the quilt comes together in no time at all. The quilt is tied with embroidery thread rather than quilted to give it that lovely country look. When finished, the quilt is 57″ × 57″—a perfect size for a picnic blanket!

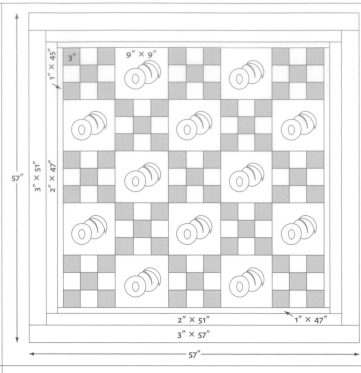

See stencils A to D on page 116

Just Peachy Picnic Quilt

CUTTING

Cut 12 9½" squares from the light yellow fabric for the peach stencils

Cut 65 3½" × 3½" squares from the bright print fabrics for the nine-patch blocks

Cut 52 3½" × 3½" squares from the light print fabrics for the nine-patch blocks

Cut 5 strips 1½" wide, selvage to selvage, from the green print for the inner border

Cut 5 strips 2½" wide, selvage to selvage, from the bright yellow print for the middle border

Cut 6 strips 3½" wide, selvage to selvage, from the orange print for the outer border

Cut 6 strips 2½" wide across the width of the fabric from the orange print for the binding

Cut two 60" pieces, selvage to selvage, from the backing fabric

QUILT MATERIALS

Stenciled blocks: 1 yard light yellow print fabric

Nine-patch blocks: 2/3 yard bright print (pinks, corals, oranges); 2/3 yard light print (peach)

Inner border: ½ yard bright green print

Middle border: ½ yard bright yellow print

Border and binding: 1 yard orange print

Backing: 3½ yards coordinating fabric

Batting: 60" × 60"

6-ply strand embroidery floss in yellow, orange, green and brown

Two skeins each of size 5 perle cotton in medium green and bright coral

Embroidery needle for quilting; large embroidery needle for tying

STENCILING MATERIALS

11" × 15" piece of stencil plastic (available at craft stores)

Exacto knife

Acrylic paint colors orange, pumpkin, bright yellow, medium green, chocolate brown

½" stencil brush

Paper towels

Small ceramic plate

Black marking pen

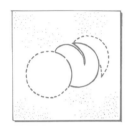
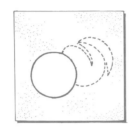
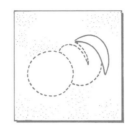
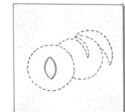

Step 1

See stencils A to D on page 116.

STENCILING

1. Trace the four stencil designs onto stencil plastic using a black marking pen. You'll have a leaf, a whole peach, a peach half, and pit.

Carefully cut out the stencils using an Exacto knife. To make placement easier while painting, trace the peach pit onto the section of the peach half that falls away when cut.

2. Place Stencil A (the whole peach) on a 9½″ light yellow fabric square, positioning as shown on the layout diagram. Pour a small amount of each of the paints onto the plate. Fold the paper towels into a 6″ blotting pad. Hold the brush in a perpendicular position and dab in the pumpkin paint. Blot on the paper towel pad to remove excess paint.

3. Still holding the brush in a perpendicular position, pounce onto the fabric, moving continuously until you have desired coverage. Next, dip the brush into the orange paint (the highlight color) and blot off any excess. Pounce along the edges. Remove the stencil and wipe it clean of any paint. Rinse the brush and blot out the moisture.

4. Repeat step 2, this time using Stencil B (peach half) and yellow paint. Use pumpkin paint as the highlight color.

5. Position stencil C (leaf), dip the brush into green paint, and blot out excess. Pounce, making darker along the edges. Remove the stencil and wipe clean. Rinse brush and blot.

6. Repeat step 4, this time using Stencil D (peach pit) and brown paint.

7. Follow steps 2 to 6 to complete the remaining blocks, then set the paint by pressing the blocks with a hot iron, both fronts and backs. Be sure to use a press cloth and protect your ironing board with a piece of muslin.

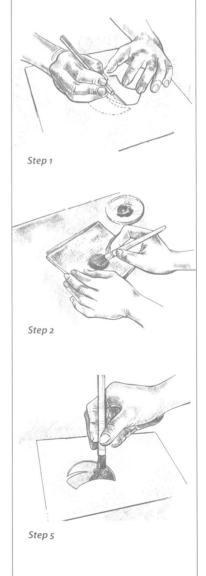

JODIE SAYS

To save time, stencil assembly-line style, painting all the blocks with Stencil A and then moving on to Stencils B, C, and D.

Step 1

Step 2

Step 5

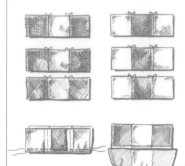

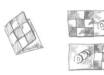

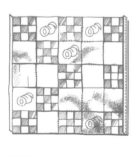

Step 3

Step 4

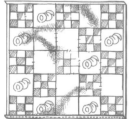

Step 5

Processing raw cotton at a huge cotton press.

All seam allowances are ¼″ unless specified otherwise.

STEP BY STEP

1. For the nine-patch blocks, begin by chain-stitching half the 3½″ squares together (see pages 84–90). Place a light square on top of a dark square, right sides together, and stitch. Without raising the pressure foot, feed another light/dark pair and stitch. You are stitching the light/dark pairs into a long chain.

2. Clip apart and add a third square, making 26 dark/light/dark strips and 13 light/dark/light strips. Press the seam allowances towards the darker fabric.

3. Match and sew the strips together in a dark/light/dark-light/dark/light-dark/light/dark sequence to form the nine-patch blocks. Press the seams open.

4. Sew the blocks together into five rows of five blocks. Sew three rows beginning with a nine-patch block and alternating with stenciled blocks across the row. Sew two rows beginning with stenciled blocks and alternating with nine-patch blocks across the row. Sew the rows together following the layout diagram on page 42.

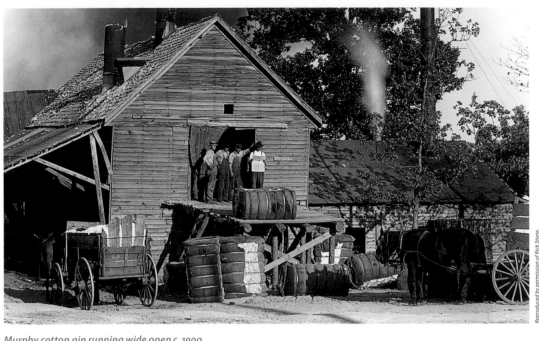

Murphy cotton gin running wide open c. 1900.

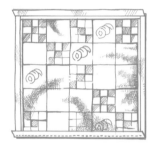

Step 5

Step 8

5. For the inner border, piece the 1½″ green strips together into one long strip. Sew to the two sides of the quilt, cutting the strip as needed. Press the seams towards the border and trim. Sew strips to the top and bottom edges, press the seams towards the border, and trim. For the middle border, repeat using the 2½″ yellow strips, then for the outer border, repeat using the 3½″ orange strips. Press the quilt top thoroughly.

6. Piece and trim the backing fabric to make a 60″ square. Sandwich the backing, batting, and quilt front and safety pin them together as instructed on page 92.(An alternative is to spray-baste them together with the special temporary fabric adhesives available from quilt and craft stores.)

7. Using two strands of the appropriate color embroidery floss, quilt around the stenciled peach motifs using a longer-than-usual stitch of about ³⁄₁₆″. See page 92 for hand quilting instructios.

8. Tie the quilt together using the large embroidery needle and perle cotton thread. Tie at every intersection of the squares, using one strand each of green and coral perle cotton threads.

9. Carefully trim the edges of the quilt sandwich then bind the quilt as instructed on pages 93–94.

Checkerboard pattern with simple stenciling.

Summer Placemats

MATERIALS

Makes two placemats
Stenciled block: 7″ × 14″ piece light yellow print fabric
Checkerboard blocks: ½ yard bright print (pinks, corals, oranges) fabrics; ½ yard light print (peach) fabric
Border and binding: ½ yard bright green print
Backing: ½ yard coordinating print
Batting: 32″ × 44″
6-ply embroidery floss in orange and green
One skein each of size 5 perle cotton in medium green and bright coral
Embroidery needle for quilting; large embroidery needle for tying
6″ × 8″ piece of stencil plastic (available at craft stores)
See the list of stenciling materials required for Just Peachy Picnic Quilt on page 42

Bring a splash of summer sunshine to your table all year round with these bright and cheerful easy-do placemats. What a wonderful gift they would make for a special friend to chase away the dull day doldrums. Luscious peaches anchor the colorful checkerboard pattern, just shouting "Look at me!" At 20″ × 14″, they are small and light enough to roll up inside your picnic quilt, too!

See stencils A to B on page 117

Summer Placemats

CUTTING *(makes 2)*

Cut 2 6½″ squares from the light yellow
   fabric for the peach stencils

Cut 20 3 1/2″ squares from the bright print
   for the checkerboard

Cut 20 3 1/2″ squares from the light print for
   the checkerboard

Cut 4 strips 1 1/2″ wide, selvage to selvage,
   from the green print for the border

Cut 4 strips 2 1/2″ wide, selvage to selvage,
   from the green print for the binding

Cut 2 pieces 20″ × 14″ for the backing

STENCILING

1. Follow step 1 of the stenciling instructions
on page 43 to prepare Stencils A and B.

2. Follow steps 2 to 4 of the stenciling
instructions on page 43 to apply the paint
onto the 6½″ yellow square of fabric. Use
stencil A (the whole peach) with pumpkin
paint then orange highlight paint; use Stencil
B with green paint. As on page 43, set the
paint by pressing with a hot iron.

❝ JODIE SAYS

To get a feel for
the stenciling
process, stencil
a complete motif
on scrap fabric
before beginning
your blocks. ❞

SWEET FRIED PIES

Makes 12 single-serving pies

Fried (that's frahd) pies are a signature Southern treat.

Pastry
3 cups all-purpose flour
1 tsp salt
¾ cup solid vegetable shortening
1 large egg
¼ cup cold water
1 tsp white vinegar

Fruit Filling
3 cups dried peaches, apricots, or apples
1½ cups water
6 tbsp sugar
¼ tsp cinnamon
¼ tsp allspice

Liquid vegetable oil for frying

1. In a medium mixing bowl, whisk the flour and salt together. Use a pastry cutter (or two knives) to cut the shortening into the flour mixture until mixture resembles coarse crumbs. Beat the egg and water together with a fork in a cup. Sprinkle the egg mixture and then the vinegar over the flour. Mix ingredients lightly with a fork until it forms a ball. If needed, add additional water by the teaspoon until mixture holds together. Wrap in plastic wrap and refrigerate.

2. Simmer the dried fruit and water in a heavy saucepan over low heat until very tender (about 45 minutes). Add additional water by the tablespoon if needed to keep the fruit from scorching. Mash slightly and stir in the sugar and spices. Cool.

3. Quarter the refrigerated pastry by cutting in half and in half again. Cut each quarter into three pieces, then form each piece into a ball. On a lightly floured surface roll the ball into a 6" circle.

4. Spoon two tablespoons of the filling onto one half of the dough circle. Dip your finger in the water and wet the edge of the circle. Fold in half and press the edges together with the prongs of a fork. Trim the pastry to neaten it up.

5. Use a 10" cast iron pan and pour oil to ½" depth. Heat to 375°F. Fry on each side until golden brown. Drain on paper towels. The pies can be sprinkled with a cinnamon/sugar mixture or powdered confectioner's sugar.

The Perfect Picnic Fare

SWEET FRIED PIES are a staple of Southern kitchens from times gone by. So full of down-home flavor, they will quickly become a family favorite—nothing at all like the poor imitations found in fast-food joints. This recipe is the real thing: an exquisitely delicious Southern take on apple pie. Oh so heavenly! Fried pies are the perfect portable dessert, tucked into your picnic basket next to the fried chicken, coleslaw, and potato salad. Or take them to your next block party or potluck dinner.

Less traditional but full of good Southern flavor is my recipe for the Peachtini. Sip one while you enjoy a sunset on the porch or serve them at your next backyard barbeque. Grilled Vidalia Onions are a tasty accompaniment to the steak, chicken, or chops you'll surely have sizzling on the grill.

PEACHTINI
Makes one serving

What better way to enjoy sunsets on the porch than with a sweet peach-flavored martini? Enjoy!

3 oz peach flavored vodka
1 oz peach schnapps
2 oz orange juice
⅓ oz Grenadine
Squeeze of lime (from wedge)

Measure ingredients into cocktail shaker. Add ice to fill halfway, shake, and strain into large martini glass.

GRILLED VIDALIA ONIONS
Makes one serving

A tasty accompaniment to steak, chicken, or chops on the grill

1 medium onion
1 bouillon cube
1 tbsp butter
Parmesan cheese (optional)

1. Peel and core the onion.

2. Place butter and boullion into the center. Sprinkle with parmesan cheese, if desired.

3. Wrap in heavy duty or doubled foil, leaving a small opening as a vent. Grill for approximately 30 minutes or until tender.

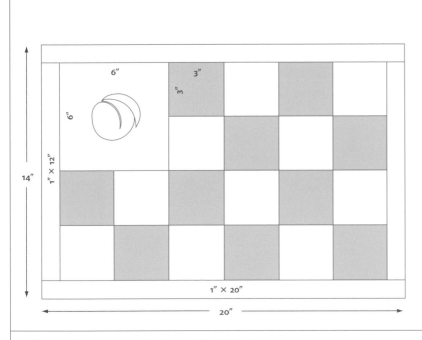

All seam allowances are ¼" unless specified otherwise

STEP BY STEP

1. For the checkerboard, chain stitch the 3½" squares together. Place a light square on top of a dark square, right sides together, and stitch. Without raising the pressure foot, feed another light/dark pair and stitch.

2. Clip apart and press seams. Sew 2 pairs together alternating dark and light squares for rows 1 and 2. Sew rows 1 and 2 together, press, and add a stenciled block to the left side. Sew 2 more rows using 3 pairs of squares for each. Sew rows together. Remember to press, press, press as you go.

3. Piece the 1½" green strips together into one long strip. Sew to the two sides of the placemat, cutting the strip as needed. Press

the seams towards the border and trim. Sew strips to top and bottom edges, press towards the border, and trim.

4. Press the placemat well. Sandwich the backing, batting, and front, then safety pin them together as instructed on page 92.

5. Quilt the stencil blocks. Using 2 strands of the appropriate color embroidery floss, quilt around the motifs using a longer-than-usual stitch of about ³⁄₁₆".

6. Tie the layers together as shown on page 45.

7. Trim the edges of the "sandwich." Bind the placemat as instructed on pages 93–94.

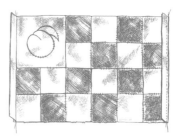

Step 2

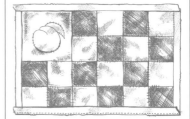

Step 3

Pack-Me-Up Cutlery Roll

MATERIALS

First checkerboard block: ⅛ yard bright print (pinks, corals, oranges) fabrics

Alternating checkerboard block and backing: ¼ yard or fat quarter of light print (peach) fabric

Border, binding, pocket, and flaps: ⅔ yard bright green print

Batting: 11" × 17"

One skein each of size 5 perle cotton in medium green and bright coral

Large embroidery needle for tying

6" × 8" piece of stencil plastic (available at craft stores)

½"-wide grosgrain ribbon (green): 1 yard

You'll always be ready for a picnic with this handy roll-up for your silverware. Just pack and go! Add the placemats and picnic quilt and you have a total ensemble for a sunny summer day.

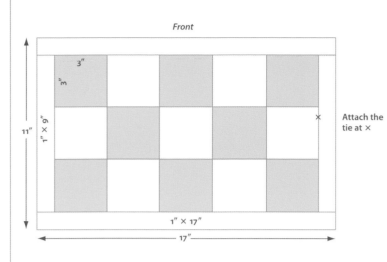

Front

3"
3"

11"

1" × 9"

1" × 17"

17"

Back

Attach the
tie at ×

Pack-Me-Up
Cutlery Roll

CUTTING

Cut 8 3½" squares from the bright print for
the checkerboard

Cut 7 3½" squares from the light print for the
checkerboard

Cut 2 strips 1½" wide, selvage to selvage, from
the green print for the borders

Cut 2 strips 2½" wide, selvage to selvage,
from the green print for the binding

Cut 1 piece 11" × 17" from the light print for
the backing

Cut 1 piece 12" × 17" from the green print for
the pockets

Cut 1 piece 12" × 16" from the green print for
the flap

STEP BY STEP

1. Follow Steps 1 to 2 of Summer Placemats
on page 49 to piece three rows of five
alternating squares into a checkerboard
pattern (omit the stenciled block). Follow the
layout diagram above.

2. Follow Steps 3 to 4 of Summer Placemats
on page 49 to add the borders.

3. Fold the pocket piece in half along the
12" side (wrong sides facing) and press. Edge-
stitch along the fold.

4. Align the pocket as shown on the layout
diagram and baste the raw edges. Make lines
of stitching through all layers to delineate
the pockets. The stitches follow the vertical
sewing lines of the checkerboard.

5. Fold the flap in half lengthwise, right
sides facing. Press, then stitch along the two
short sides. Turn right side out and press.
Edge stitch along the three seamed edges.

6. Align the flap as shown on the layout
diagram and baste the raw edge.

7. Tie the quilt together as shown on page 45
using one strand each of the green and coral
perle cotton.

8. Trim the edges of the "sandwich." Bind
the roll as instructed on pages 95–96. Sew the
middle of the ribbon tie to the front of the
roll, as shown on the layout diagram. Take
care not to catch the flap.

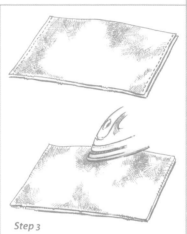

Step 3

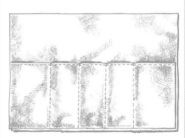

Step 4

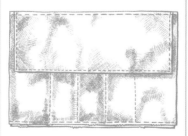

Step 5

Scrapbook Pillows

What better way to combine the fun of scrap-booking with your love of fabric! These picture-postcard pillows borrow the charm of vintage postcards and transform them into home-dec delights. Using photo transfer and a color inkjet copier, the image is copied onto the fabric and sewn. The fabric is then sewn into an accent pillow.

MATERIALS

Photo transfer fabric: 9½″ × 5½″

Green fabric for insert around photo: 4″ × 9½″

Light beige fabric for side inner border: 10″ × 10″

Brown fabric for outer border: 10″ × 15″

Backing: 12½″ × 16½″

12″ × 16″ pillow form

Your favorite postcard or photograph!

Step 2

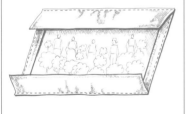

Step 3

All seam allowances are ¼″ unless specified otherwise.

Scrapbook Pillows

STEP BY STEP

1. Using the black and white setting on your copier, make a test copy of the postcard to size or enlarge as desired (my postcard image measures 6″ × 10″). When you have found the correct setting, copy the image in color onto photo transfer fabric.

2. Cut the green fabric into four 1″-wide strips. Fold in half lengthwide and press. Baste the strips to the top and bottom edges of the fabric photo. Trim even with the raw edges of the photo. Baste the strips to the sides of the fabric photo. Trim.

3. From the light beige fabric, cut four 2½″-wide strips. Sew to the top and bottom edges of the fabric photo, including the green insert strips in the stitching. Trim even with the raw edges of the fabric photo. Repeat for the sides.

> **JODIE SAYS**
>
> I love these unique, everyday reminders of my visit to Cotton Country. ,

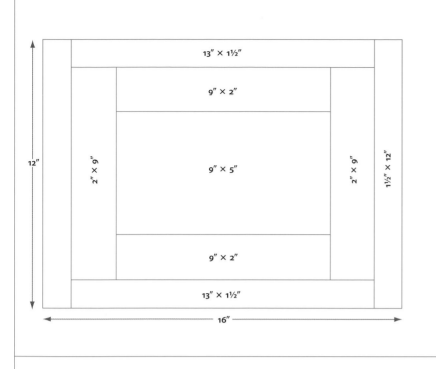

13" × 1½"

9" × 2"

2" × 9"

9" × 5"

2" × 9"

1½" × 12"

12"

9" × 2"

13" × 1½"

16"

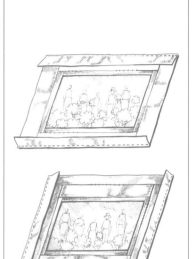

Step 4

Step 5

4. From the brown fabric, cut four 2"-wide strips. Sew to the top and bottom edges of the light beige inner border. Trim even with the raw edges of the fabric photo. Repeat for the sides.

5. Trim the completed pillow front to measure 12½" × 16½" and place right side up on your work surface.

6. Place the pillow back piece on top, right side down, with raw edges matching those of the pillow front. Pin. Sew, leaving a 6" gap in the stitching to insert the pillow form. Turn right side out. Insert the pillow form and hand stitch the opening closed.

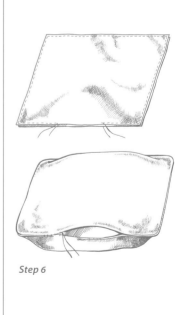

Step 6

Cotton Boll Redwork Pillow

As a designer, I am always on the look-out for unusual design motifs, and the cotton boll certainly fits the bill. When I visited Cotton Country, I was struck by the unusual shape and texture of cotton bolls, dotting the fields as far as the eye can see. The cotton flower has five large petals that vary in shade from bright white to creamy white to light rose. When the petals fall, they leave behind the hard brown capsule or "boll", which bursts open to reveal masses of downy fibers, ready for picking.

JUST HOW BIG IS A BALE OF COTTON?

A standard bale is 55″ tall, 28″ wide, and 21″ thick. It weighs in at a mighty 480 pounds. Of course, with a single bale, you can make 325 pairs of jeans. The seeds left over from making that bale produce enough oil to cook nearly 6,000 snack-size bags of potato chips!

All seam allowances are ¼" unless specified otherwise. See stencil on page 117

Cotton Boll Redwork Pillow

STEP BY STEP

1. Cut the muslin into one 18½" square and five 6½" squares. From the dark red fabric, cut two 12½" × 18½" pieces for the pillow back, then two 7½" squares for the nine-patch blocks. From the light red fabric, cut two 7½" squares for the nine-patch blocks.

2. Transfer the cotton boll stencils onto the muslin squares. Using a chain stitch, embroider the motifs, following the directions on page 91.

3. To make the nine-patch blocks, position the dark squares on top of the light squares, right sides facing and matching the raw edges. For each set, stitch two opposite sides together. Cut 2½" in from the raw edges on the sides you sewed. Press the seam allowances open or toward the dark fabric. Stitch the two pieces you just cut away to the joined strips, creating one dark-light-dark strip and one light-dark-light strip. Press the seam allowances open or toward the dark strip.

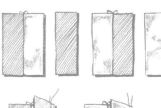

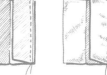

Step 3

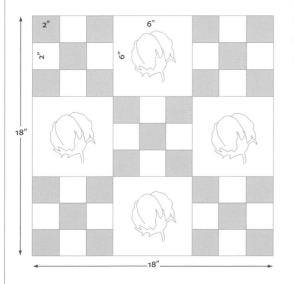

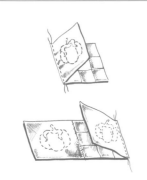

Step 4

Three generations of one family picking cotton. The child in the basket has the job of tamping down the cotton before it is taken to the wagon and then on to the gin.

Step 5

4. Cut into three 2½″ segments. Match and sew the strips together to create the nine-patch blocks.

5. Lay out the nine-patch squares and the embroidered squares for the pillow top and sew them together in rows following the layout diagram on page 57. Press the seam allowances toward the nine-patch squares as you go. Sew the rows together.

6. Sandwich the muslin backing, batting, and pillow front as instructed on page 94. Quilt the layers together, outlining each cotton boll and quilting about ¼″ inside each muslin square. Quilt diagonally across the nine patches.

7. Press under 1″ along one longer edge of each pillow back. Turn under ¼″. Topstitch. Place the pillow front right-side-up on your work surface. Place the pillow back pieces on top, right sides down, with the finished edges overlapping at the center and their raw edges even with those of the pillow front. Pin. Sew all the way around, overlapping the beginning stitching at the end. Turn the pillow right side out. (See also the drawings for step 6 of Cotton Boll Basket Pillow on page 55.)

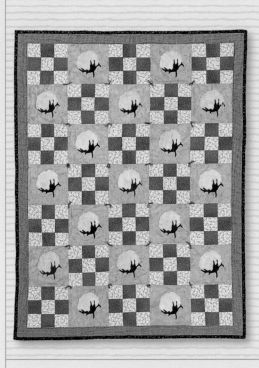

From Pillow to Quilt

I LOVED MY NINE-PATCH PILLOW so much that I decided to expand the design into a lap quilt. The nine patch blocks were made with the exact same strip piecing method used for the pillow. I made a total of 18 blocks. To recreate the motif, I used white and brown acrylic fabric paints to stencil the cotton boll design. I traced the redwork design to make a cotton boll stencil (see page 117). The design was transferred to stencil plastic, then painted onto seventeen 6½" squares of light green fabric. (Use a light touch—and be sure to test on scrap fabric first. For extra help on stenciling and stenciling materials, see page 43.) As well as quilting the layers together around the cotton boll motifs, I used embroidery floss to "tie" the layers at each block intersection (see also page 45).

To make my 34" × 46" lap quilt, you will need ⅔ yard of light green fabric for the stenciled blocks, ½ yard each of green print and beige print for the nine-patch blocks, ½ yard brown check fabric for the borders, and ⅜ yard of dark brown fabric for the binding. You'll also need 1¼ yards of backing fabric and a 40" × 50" piece of batting. See pages 92–95 to assemble the quilt and add a hanging sleeve.

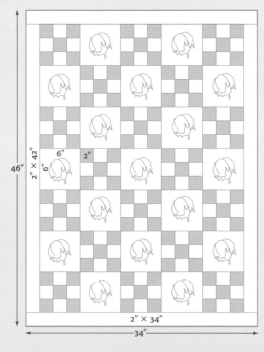

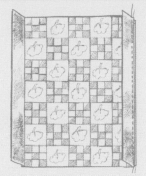

Add the side borders

Add the top and bottom borders

Tie-bind

Snip and knot the ties

MULES IN ACTION AT
Westville Village

THE STORY OF COTTON would not be complete without a visit to Westville Village in Lumpkin, Georgia, where the power behind the ginning of cotton is . . . none other than our four-hoofed friend, the mule. Far from the moonlight-and-magnolia South, Westville Village, is an authentic recreation of a hardworking pre-Civil War town. It is a picture-window into daily life across a variety of social classes and Southern trades. From a crude log cabin built in the 1830s to the graceful columned home of a prosperous merchant, each of the thirty-one authentic structures along the village's dirt streets has been restored and outfitted with determined dedication to its original form. Only three buildings were added to complete the village, the rest (built between 1836 and 1859) were moved to this location from surrounding towns where they had been slated for demolition. Today, Westville Village holds the largest collection south of Williamsburg of antebellum homes, shops, churches, and other structures.

Walking through the streets of Westville, it is easy to imagine that you have been transported back through time. Volunteers in authentic period dress populate the village, where they demonstrate everyday tasks and skills from a period when life depended upon animal power and human handicrafts. This is a time of blacksmithing, candle-making, white oak basket weaving, and, of course, farmhouse cooking. There is even hand-thrown, salt-glazed pottery firing in a groundhog kiln. I joined Bobbie at her quilt frame, helped Veronica and her two daughters dye fabric outdoors at the MacDonald House, and wove a few rows on Jeanine's large loom. After all that grueling 19th century labor,

Photograph by Mike Haskey

OPPOSITE *The Bryant House, circa 1831, is one of the grander homes at Westville Village.* ABOVE *A girl in period dress overlooks the corn and cotton patch.*

Photograph by Mike Haskey

Photograph by Mike Haskey

LEFT *Hot coats are shoveled on top of Dutch ovens to bake biscuits the old-fashioned way.* ABOVE *Busy hands pat out biscuits one by one for a hearty breakfast.*

I headed to The Kiser House where delicious sausage, biscuits, gingerbread, and lemonade were waiting for visitors. It's all made the old-fashioned way and most delicious!

Special events in Westville Village are truly unique treats: a fiddle contest, period baseball, a reenactment of a Yellow Fever outbreak, and an 1850s wedding in the town church are part of the full year-round calendar.

I waited the entire year to witness Westville Village's premier event: the Harvest Festival. In particular, I wanted to see Henry Lynch harness mules to the power train for Westville's Bagley Cotton Gin. Starting and stopping by voice command, the mules walk in a circle on the ground floor of the gin. They are hitched to long beams which, when put in motion, turn gears attached to belts powering the gin. As the raw cotton is placed into the cotton gin, the moving saw-like blades pull the lint from the cotton seed. The lint is blown through a shoot into the adjacent lint room while the seeds fall into a storage bin beneath the gin. In its heyday, the gin could produce enough cotton lint for two bales of cotton daily. The Bagley Cotton Gin is the first mule-powered cotton gin to be restored in America, and is one of only three mule-powered gins known to be still in operation.

The *piece de resistance* at Westville for a cotton lover like me is the animal-powered baler, the only working baler in the U.S. A sack of lint cotton is carried from the lint room of the gin up the steep steps of the baler and stuffed into a large wooden box, accessed from the elevated platform. Above this box, a massive wooden screw is situated horizontally. Attached to the top of the screw are huge timbers which jut out over the baler and angle to the ground where yoked oxen slowly crank the screw by walking in a circle around the baler. As they do so, the screw tightens and forces a big block of wood into the box. This compresses the cotton lint, thus forming a bale of cotton. It takes one oxen and one man to produce two bales of cotton in a day. Compare that to the Tanner's modern gin's production of 900 bales daily!

Photograph by Mike Haskey

ABOVE *Jeanette Greene works at the warping board measuring warp threads to ready a loom for weaving.*

OPPOSITE *David Corbett stands at his anvil in the Bealer Forge.*

TWILIGHT HOUR *in the* CABIN

The front porch on Southern homes did more than welcome friends for a glass of sweet iced tea. After rising before dawn to a long day on the farm and having enjoyed the rewards of their labor at the supper table, the family gathered on the front porch to rest and tell tales.

A family socializes on the front porch.
Documenting the American South (http://docsouth.unc.edu), The University
of North Carolina at Chapel Hill Libraries, North Carolina Collection

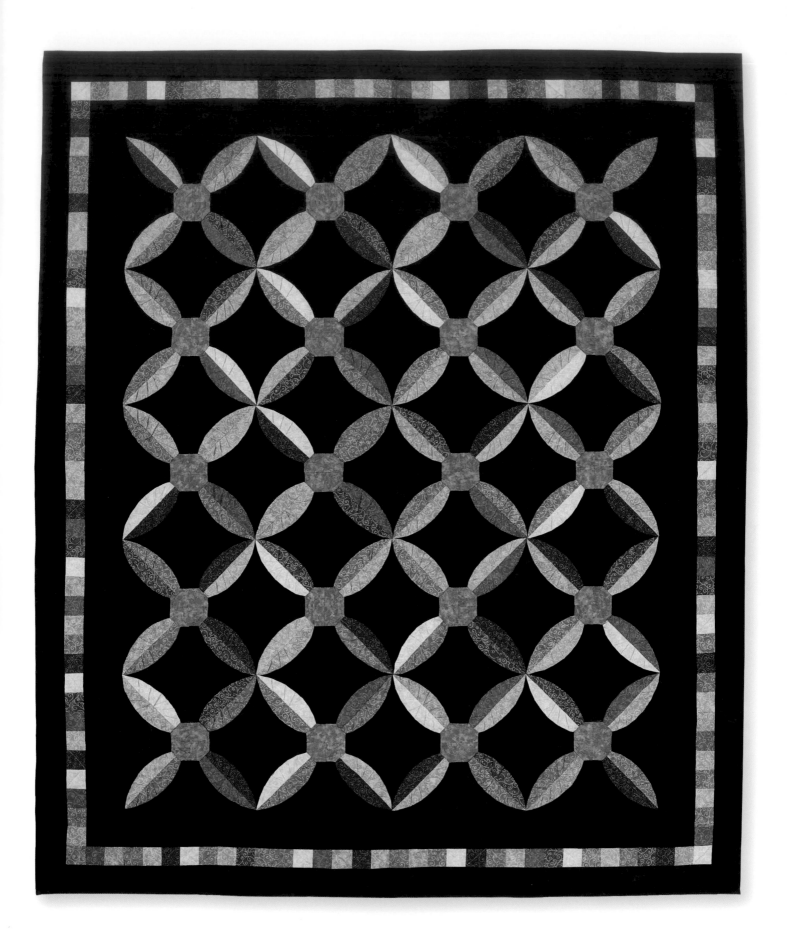

Mule's Ear Bed Quilt

This colorful Mule's Ear Quilt, set against a nighttime sky, was inspired by a striped-pieced block pattern of the same name. For our quilt, I chose to use my stitch-and-pleat paper-piecing technique, which makes curves a breeze. The black background and bright colors of the Moda Marbles and Moda Swirls fabrics sure make those ears pop! And since most of the pattern pieces are "rough-cut" prior to paper piecing, this project is a great way to use up lots of colorful fabric scraps. When finished, the quilt measures 74″ × 88″—perfect for a full size bed!

A MULE DITTY

*"On mules we find two legs behind
And two we find before·
We stand behind before we find
What the two behind be for!
When we're behind the two behind
We find what these be for—
So stand before the two behind
Behind the two before!"*

ANONYMOUS

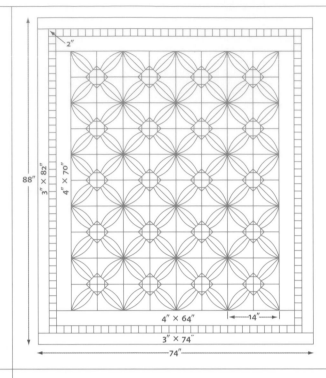

MATERIALS

Mule ears: 1 yard each of bright
   fabrics in green, lemon lime,
   red, blue, purple, orange,
   turquoise, and pink
Center units: ¾ yard light brown
   fabric
Background and binding:
   4¼ yards marbled black or
   alternate dark fabric
Batting: 78″ × 92″
Backing fabric: 6 yards

Mule's Ear Bed Quilt

CUTTING

From the black or dark background fabric,
cut:

Eight 2½″ strips selvage to selvage for the
   binding

Two 4½″ × 70½″ pieces for inner side
   border

Two 4½″ × 64½″ pieces for inner top and
   bottom border

Two 3½″ × 82½″ pieces for the outer side
   border

Two 3½″ × 74½″ pieces for the outer top
   and bottom border

From the multi-colored bright fabrics, cut
   and piece 146 2½″ squares for the middle
   border

The brown center units are paper pieced

PAPER PIECING GUIDELINES

When paper piecing, always begin by cutting
the fabric for each patch larger than you
think it needs to be. Add about ½″ around
all sides. (Once you develop an eye for how
much you need, you can be more economical
with your fabric.)

   The printed side of the pattern is always
on the wrong, or back, side of the finished
block. When sewing, the printed side of the
block faces up, so that you can see the sewing
lines. The fabric is underneath the paper.

   Once you have cut a fabric patch and
matched it up to the paper-piecing pattern,
you may wish to place a pin through the
fabric and paper to hold them in place. Better
yet, dab each with a fabric glue stick; when

> ❝ **JODIE SAYS**
>
> Always leave paper foundations in place until after the quilt top is completed. Blocks are easier to align this way and will not become distorted by the tearing process. ❞

All seam allowances are ¼" unless specified otherwise. See templates A to C on pages 118–119

the quilt is washed, the glue will wash out! This way you won't have to worry about the pin getting in the way of your stitching.

As with traditional piecing, always position the two patches to be sewn together so that right sides are facing. The only difference with paper piecing is that a piece of paper lies on top of the two fabric pieces and you sew through the paper along the marked seam line.

Set your machine stitch length to 1.5. This shortened stitch length will make the job of removing the paper from your blocks easier, thanks to the perforations added by the needle going in and out of the paper more often.

When you are ready to sew and have the block under the pressure foot of your sewing machine, the lower patch number (the one you just sewed) will be to your left, and the patch you are adding will be to your right. The bulk of the fabric will extend out to your left. Keeping this simple rule in mind makes the sewing go much more smoothly.

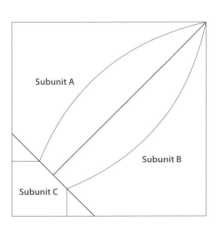

BOLL WEEVIL HUMOR!

"Two boll weevils grew up in South Carolina. One went to Hollywood and became a famous actor. The other stayed behind in the cotton fields and never amounted to much. The second one, naturally, became known as the lesser of two weevils."

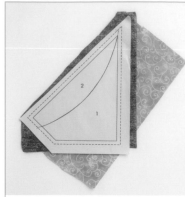

Step 4

Step 5

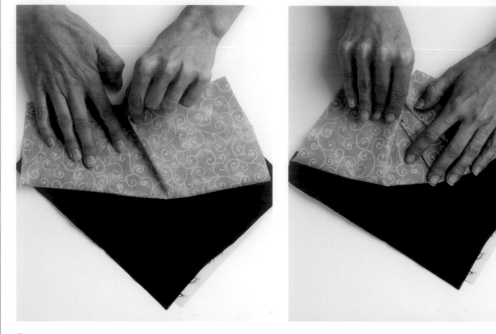

Step 6

Step 7

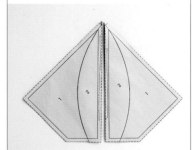

Step 8

STEP BY STEP

1. Make 80 paper copies of each of the templates for Subunits A, B, and C (I use newsprint). Remove any extraneous blank paper by cutting it away about ½″ outside the dashed lines—just enough so that you don't have a lot of extra paper in your way.

Subunits A and B

2. Start paper piecing Subunit A. For Patch 1, rough-cut a piece of black fabric, making it about ½″ larger all around than the pattern piece. Place the fabric patch on the unprinted side of the paper pattern for Subunit A so that it easily covers the entire area of Patch 1. Pin to hold in place. (Make sure the wrong side of the fabric faces the unprinted side of the paper.)

3. For Patch 2, rough-cut a piece of colored fabric, again generously larger than the area of the patch itself. Place the fabric so its right side faces the right side of the Patch 1 fabric, with ¼″ or more of the fabric extending into the area of Patch 2.

4. Shorten your stitch length to 1.5 (or 15 stitches per inch, depending upon your sewing machine brand). Start stitching three or four stitches before the marked sewing line. Sew along the curved line and past it, extending three stitches or so. Flip up fabric Patch 2 to be sure it covers the entire Patch 2 area of the paper pattern.

5. Trim the seam allowance to ¼″. Open out and turn right side up.

6. Make tucks in the remaining colored fabric, folding the tucks toward the center of the curve to make them lie flat. Fold a total of six tucks, three on each side, placing a pin in each tuck as you go.

7. With the marked side of the paper facing up, machine-baste between the dashed-line and solid-line seam markings to secure the pleats, removing pins as you go. (For faster paper removal later, choose the longest basting stitch possible—you'll be thankful when you remove the stitches!)

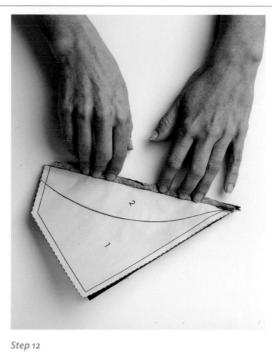

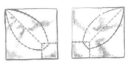
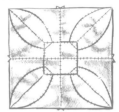
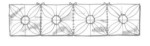

Step 13

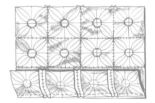
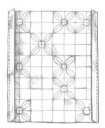

Step 14

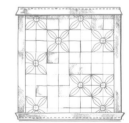

Step 15

Step 16

8. Position Subunit A fabric side down (marked paper side up) on a cutting mat. Using a rotary cutter and ruler, trim the edges of the block along the dashed lines. This leaves a ¼″ seam allowance all around the block. Make sure you cut through the paper foundation and fabric. Leave the paper foundation in place and set aside.

9. Repeat steps 2 to 8 until all A and B subunits are complete.

Subunits C

10. Using brown fabric for Patch 1 and background fabric for Patch 2, begin making Subunits C in the same way. Note that you are sewing on a straight line, not a curved line, so steps 6 to 7 do not apply.

BLOCK ASSEMBLY

11. To assemble the block, stitch a Subunit A to a Subunit B, using pins through the corners as shown to match your points perfectly. Sew along the printed line on the paper.

12. Remove the paper from the seam allowances. Press the seam allowances open. In the same way, add Subunit C.

13. Stitch four units together to form a block. Remove paper from the seam allowances as you sew them and press all seams open.

QUILT ASSEMBLY

14. Stitch the blocks into five sets of four blocks each. Stitch the sets together.

15. Stitch the longer inner border pieces to the sides of the quilt top. Press the seams toward the border. Stitch the remaining inner border pieces to the top and bottom of the quilt. Press the seams toward the border.

16. Stitch the 2½″ squares of colored fabrics into two sets of 41 squares each for the sides of the quilt and two sets of 32 squares each for the top and bottom of the quilt. Press the seam allowances to one side.

Winter Warmers

SOUTHERN SPOON BREAD

Serves 8

A super easy version of a traditional southern side dish.

3 tbsp salted butter, plus more for pan and serving
2 cups water
1 cup yellow cornmeal
1 tsp salt
3 large eggs, well beaten
1 cup whole milk

1. Preheat oven to 375°F. Lightly butter a 7-cup soufflé dish or casserole.

2. Place 2 cups water in a medium saucepan over medium-high heat. Bring to a boil. Slowly add cornmeal stirring constantly until thick and smooth.

3. Remove from the heat. Add butter and salt and let stand until lukewarm. Add eggs and milk.

4. Beat well for one minute, then pour into prepared baking dish. Bake until golden brown, about 35 minutes. Serve hot with butter.

Between the cotton harvest ending in October and the planting of corn, a Southern staple, in March, farm life slowed just a bit with winter. Meat was prepared and cured, repairs made to fences, buildings, and gear, and time allowed for social life, often revolving around church—and involving covered-dish dinners.

Frosty Southern mornings called for hot and hearty table fare. A classic hot dish, spoon bread is a custard-like corn bread. Because it is soft, it is generally eaten with a spoon, hence its name. A staple at Thomas Jefferson's Monticello and known to have been served at George Washington's home in Mount Vernon, spoon bread was a regular on every Southern table.

Murphy Cotton Gin, winter, c. 1901.

17. Stitch the shorter sets of squares to the top and bottom of the quilt. Press the seam allowances toward the black border piece. Stitch the longer sets of squares to the sides of the quilt. Press the seam allowances toward the black border.

18. Stitch the longer outer border pieces to the sides of the quilt top. Press the seams toward the border. Stitch the remaining outer border pieces to the top and bottom of the quilt. Press the seams toward the border.

FINISHING

19. Cut the backing fabric into two equal pieces, remove the selvage edges, and sew together so the length runs horizontally. Following the directions on page 92, sandwich your quilt.

20. Quilt in the black areas using a large meander, quilt a spiral in the brown center of each group of mule ears, and quilt diagonally across each colored border square.

21. Turn to pages 93–94 for directions to bind your quilt.

Step 17

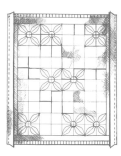

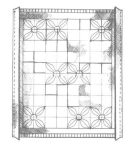

Step 18

*Quick cut-and-fuse
appliqué pillow case
with ruffle edge*

Farm Kids Sham

This sleepy-time pillow sham is sure to bring sweet dreams of life on the farm. It will quickly become your special child's favorite for naptime or for cozy reading at twilight. The figures are fused onto a striped background and surrounded by simple ruffles. Measuring 33″ × 27″ (including the ruffle), the sham is just right for standard sized bed pillows.

MATERIALS

Blue striped fabric for pillow top,
   cut 2: 20½ " × 26½ " each
Muslin for pillow top lining:
   20½" × 26½ "
Batting: 20½" × 26½ "
Pillow back fabric, cut 2:
   20½" × 17½ " each
Ruffle fabric: 1 yard fabric of your
   choice
Doll bodies, cut 3: 10"x 10" each
Doll hair, cut 2: 4" × 4" each
Dresses, cut 2: 5" × 6" each
Overalls: 5" × 7" cotton or
   lightweight denim, plus
   1¼ " × 1¼ " red scrap for patch
Hat: 3" × 5"
Fusible web: 1 yard
Machine embroidery thread or
   hand embroidery floss
Buttons

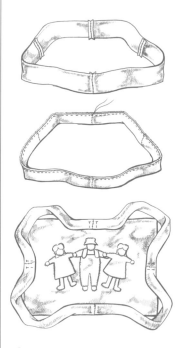

Step 2

Step 4

All seam allowances are ¼" unless specified otherwise. See templates A to E on pages 110–111

STEP BY STEP

1. Prepare the fusible appliqués for all three dolls and fuse them in place, as directed on page oo. Blanket stitch the edges by hand or machine, as on page 91. Sew buttons in place.

2. Right side down, place the lining fabric on a flat surface. Smooth the batting on top, matching edges. Lay the pillow top, right side up on top, matching all raw edges. Use safety pins to pin the layers together.

3. Machine quilt all around the dolls. All across the pillow, machine quilt vertical lines about 1¼" apart, or use the stripes printed on the fabric as a quilting guide.

4. From the ruffle fabric, cut four strips selvage to selvage, each 7½ " wide. Trim off the selvage edges. Seam the strips together to form a continuous loop. Press the seams open. Press in half lengthwise. Using a long machine stitch, gather-stitch the raw edges. Match and pin one ruffle seam to the halfway

AN UNLIKELY HERO

Perhaps the world's only monument honoring an agricultural pest, Enterprise Alabama's Boll Weevil Monument was erected in 1919 and has been a tourist attraction ever since.

In 1892 the Mexican boll weevil, a voracious little beetle, ate its way across the Mexican border into Texas. It munched through the cotton-producing lands of the South, feeding on the silky fibers inside the seed pods of the cotton plant. Bewildered farmers were unable to pay their debts, squeezing merchants who had loaned seed and fertilizer for planting crops.

Fearing doom on the horizon, a few forward-thinking citizens of the city of Enterprise, Alabama, traveled north to find a new crop that would ease their reliance on cotton. A strain of peanut—the North Carolina Runner—was selected, and that same year one local farmer harvested a crop worth $8,000, much to the envy of his cotton-growing neighbors who had netted a mere ten percent of their pre-boll weevil harvests. Enterprise quickly switched from cotton to peanuts, selling over a million bushels in 1917, worth over $5 million.

Proffered as a joke, Roscoe Owen Fleming told a friend that the boll weevil had done so much for Enterprise that they ought to erect a monument to the insect. The statue, ordered from Italy, was dedicated in 1919. On its base is the following inscription:

"IN PROFOUND APPRECIATION OF THE BOLL WEEVIL AND WHAT IT HAS DONE AS THE HERALD OF PROSPERITY THIS MONUMENT WAS ERECTED BY THE CITIZENS OF ENTERPRISE, COFFEE COUNTY, ALABAMA"

Step 4

point of each side of the pillow top. Pull up on the basting stitches and adjust the gathers neatly to match the ruffle to the pillow top. Baste in place.

5. Press under ¼" on one long edge of each pillow back piece. Press under another 1". Topstitch. Right sides facing the pillow top, arrange the back pieces so their finished edges overlap in the middle portion of the pillow and their three raw edges line up with the raw edges of the pillow top. Stitch all the way around.

6. Turn right side out. Press.

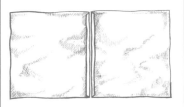

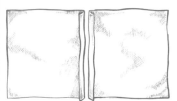

 **JODIE SAYS**
Insert the pillow in the sham and place it on your bed. Sweet dreams! **,**

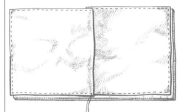

Step 5

Soft knitted velour fabric for the body pairs with regular fleece for the hooves and muzzle.

Sassy Mule

MATERIALS
Body: ⅓ yard furry fleece
Hooves: ⅛ yard regular fleece
Mane and tail: ball of yarn
Polyester fiberfill stuffing
Two 9 mm safety eyes or ⅜"
    buttons
Straw hat
Silk flowers for hat

Who can resist that sweet face? Not I! In fact my visit to Westville Village sparked quite a mule-themed creative frenzy; or did you already notice the number of mule projects in *Quilting with Jodie in Cotton Country?* Many fabrics are appropriate for the mule, Our mule stands tall at 9" high by 10" long.

Step 2

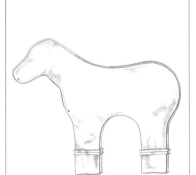

Step 4

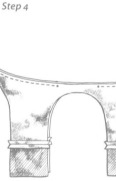

All seam allowances are ¼" unless specified otherwise. See templates on pages 120–122

STEP BY STEP

1. Pin the templates pieces to your fabrics with the arrows following the grain of the fabric. (Note: templates already include ¼" seam allowance.) Cut out the pieces. Transfer all dots and other markings to the wrong side of the fabric.

2. Right sides facing, stitch two ear pieces together. Repeat for the other two pieces. Turn them right sides out. Fold in half and baste the bottom edges together to secure.

3. Right sides facing, stitch the hooves to the bottoms of each of the legs.

4. Right sides facing, stitch the body sides together from the dot A at the chest to dot B

at the nose, backstitching at the beginning and end of the stitching.

5. Right sides facing, stitch the underbody pieces together at the underbody center, leaving an opening between the dots for turning and stuffing.

6. Right sides facing, pin and stitch the underbody to the body sides at the front of the mule, from dot A (marked on template) to the bottom of the hooves. Stitch the underbody to the body sides at the underside of the body from hoof to hoof. Stitch the underbody to the body sides from the bottom of the hooves to dot C.

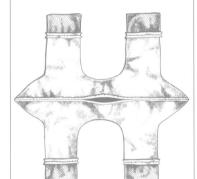

Step 5

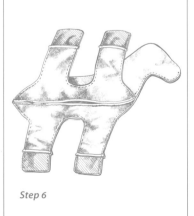

Step 6

7-UP POUND CAKE

Cake
1 cup butter, softened
½ cup shortening
3 cups sugar
1 tsp vanilla extract
5 eggs at room temperature
3 cups all-purpose flour
½ tsp salt
1 cup 7-UP

Glaze
¼ cup 7-UP
½ cup sugar

1. Preheat the oven to 325°F. Grease and flour a 10" tube or a bundt pan.

2. Beat the butter, shortening, sugar, and vanilla extract in the bowl of an electric mixer until light and fluffy (about 5 minutes).

3. Add the eggs, one at a time, beating well after each addition and scraping down the sides before adding the next egg.

4. Combine the flour and salt in a separate bowl and add alternately with the cup of 7-UP to the butter mixture, starting and ending with the dry ingredients.

5. Spoon the batter into the prepared pan. Bake for 1 hour 35 minutes or until a cake tester comes out clean. Cool in the pan on a wire rack for 10 minutes, then invert onto a serving plate and remove the baking pan.

6. While the cake is cooling, make the glaze by stirring together the ¼ cup 7 UP and the ½ cup sugar in a small saucepan. Bring to a boil over medium heat and boil for 2 to 3 minutes or until the sugar is completely dissolved. Using a toothpick, poke holes in the top of the warm cake. Spoon the glaze over the cake. Cool completely before serving.

Sweet Suppertime Surprises

MANY A CHILD RECALLS happy hours perched on the kitchen stool "helping" grandma mix, beat, and fold eggs, butter, flour, sugar and local farm products such as pecans and black-berries into delectable sweets. Numerous Southern recipes have passed down through the generations; pecan pie, red velvet cake and pralines are now well-loved throughout Cotton Country. Some are still found almost exclusively in the South.

With its sweet and crunchy crust, the 7-UP Pound Cake is a decidedly Southern version of a perpetual favorite. Our recipe has been around for years, and for good reason—it is delicious. The glaze creates a sugary—but not too sweet—crust that encases the pound cake, much like the glaze on a honey-dipped donut. The cake makes a great base for strawberry shortcake. Simpler still, sugar some raspberries a few hours before serving, spoon the juices on slices of cake, and add berries.

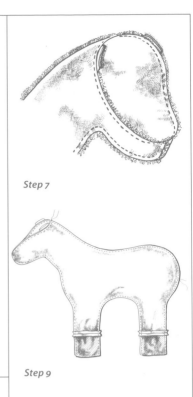

Step 7

Step 9

JODIE SAYS

Rocking chairs and porch swings are guaranteed stress relievers and as it is said in the South, set an old person in them and rocking chairs become history lessons.

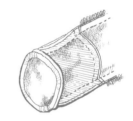

Step 10

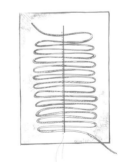

Step 12

Step 14

7. Pin the ears to the body sides at dots D, with the folded opening toward the front of the mule. Baste in place. Matching dots E on the body sides to dot E on the face front, and dots B at the tip of the nose, pin and then stitch the face front to the body sides, including the ears in the seam.

8. Make holes for the eyes at the dots on the head sides. Install the eyes.

9. Stitch the body sides together along the top of the mule from dot E at the back of the head to dot C at the tail.

10. Right sides facing, stitch the hoof bottoms to each of the hooves. Turn the mule right side out.

11. Start stuffing at a back hoof, packing golf ball-size pieces of stuffing firmly in place. Stuff the hindquarters. Next, start at the muzzle and work down the neck. Once the mule is stuffed check to make sure he can stand. If not, add more stuffing. Ladder stitch the opening closed. (Use a heavy thread,

such as quilting thread, or dental floss, which will hold up well for this stitching.)

12. For the mane, draw a 3″ line on a piece of paper. Loop the yarn back and forth along the line and perpendicular to it forming loops about 1″ on each side, stitching along the line, forming the loops just ahead of your stitching as you go. Tear the paper from the stitching. Hand-stitch the line of stitching to the seam at the mule's neck, from his withers to his poll.

13. Cut about forty 18″ lengths of yarn. Tie them together at the center with a piece of yarn. Braid them together for about 4″ and secure with a piece of yarn. Trim raw ends. Stitch the tail in place.

14. Cut holes in the hat so that the ears can slip through. Decorate it with craft flowers, then pop the hat on the mule's head.

A charming crayon embroidery— nothing could be simpler!

Goodnight Mules Crayon Embroidery

MATERIALS
Muslin: 19" × 20"
Box of 64 crayons
6-ply embroidery floss, black
#2 pencil or blue water-erase pen
Size 8 embroidery needle
Picture frame: 15" × 18"

Remember the childhood fun of coloring with crayons? Indulge yourself in a box of bright colors and bring back those early memories with this sweet project. The mules are "painted." or colored, just as a child would color them. They are then set with an iron, and outlined in a simple running embroidery stitch. You can turn your creation into a pillow cover, or frame it for the bedroom wall, as we did.

See pattern on pages 105–106

STEP-BY-STEP

1. Place the pattern on a light box or tape it to a window. Place the muslin over it. Using a #2 pencil or a blue water-erase pen, trace the design onto the muslin. Draw a border around the rectangular design, about ½″ away from the edge of the pattern.

2. Place the traced muslin on a layer or two of other fabric and color with crayons. Start lightly—you can always add more color. For even coloring, work in a circular motion.

This will help eliminate direction lines and help you shade.

3. Sandwich the muslin between two sheets of plain paper. With your iron on the cotton setting, press to set the colors.

4. Using two strands of embroidery floss and a running stitch, outline the design as instructed on page 91.

5. Frame the picture.

JODIE SAYS

Crayola water soluble markers are great for marking needle-point designs. I tested to see if the markings wash out. Sure do, like magic!

JODIE'S PRIMER *on* QUILTMAKING

The following are skills you will need to complete the projects in *Quilting with Jodie in Cotton Country*. They range from techniques that are common to all types of quilting—such as rotary cutting, strip piecing, and sandwiching the quilt—to newer methods—such as cut-and-fuse appliqué or curved paper piecing—that are specific to projects in the book. Since every quilter I know keeps a collection of good books at hand to help her in times of need, I've including a list of some of my favorites to add to your library. They will provide you with extra instruction on key techniques.

BOOKSHELF, ETC.

Hone your quilting skills with these great books:

Beyer, Jinny. *Quiltmaking by Hand: Simple Stitches, Exquisite Quilts*. Elmhurst, IL (Chicago): Breckling Press, 2004

Gaudynski, Diane. *Guide to Machine Quilting*. Paducah, KY: American Quilting Society, 2002

Hargrave, Harriet. *Mastering Machine Applique: The Complete Guide*. Lafayette, CA: C & T Publishing, 2001

Noble, Maurine. *Machine Quilting Made Easy*. Bothell, WA: That Patchwork Place, 1994

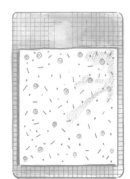

Step 1

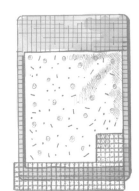

Step 2

Step 3

Rotary Cutting

You will need a cutting mat, rotary cutter, and rotary cutting rulers for the projects in this book. These are among the basic tools needed for quilting. I suggest a 6″ × 24″ clear rotary cutting ruler and a 10½″ or larger square ruler.

The object in rotary cutting is to make straight, even cuts as close to the fabric grain as possible. This way squares and rectangles are cut on the lengthwise and crosswise grain, assuring that they will not distort as they would if cut with bias edges.

1. On the cutting mat, fold the fabric in half lengthwise, aligning the selvage edges, with the raw edges to your right and fold closest to you on your left.

2. Place the square ruler along the folded edge, making sure it is aligned with the fold. Place the 6″ × 24″ ruler next to the square ruler, butting the edges and having the long ruler cover the uneven raw edges of the fabric.

3. Remove the square ruler and make a clean cut along the edge of the longer ruler.

CUTTING STRIPS

To cut a strip, align the just clean-cut edge of the fabric with the desired marking on the ruler and cut.

CUTTING SQUARES

Some of the projects in this book require nine-patch blocks or checkerboards. To make them, rather than cut individual squares and piece them together, first cut strips of each fabric, seam them together, press, and then cut the strips into units.

For a project that requires, for instance, finished (sewn) squares of 4″ × 4″, you will need to add in a ¼″ allowance all the way around, which means you will start by cutting a strip that is 4½″ wide. Next, cross-cut the strip into 4½″ squares.

Machine Piecing

SEWING A ¼″ SEAM ALLOWANCE

Many sewing machines come equipped with a presser that measures ¼″ from the stitching line to the right edge of the foot. Test your machine by sewing a sample and measuring the seam allowance. If it is not ¼″, place a piece of masking tape on your machine to mark the ¼″ seam allowance.

CHAIN PIECING

Save time and thread by sewing your patches together assembly line fashion. Place the

 **JODIE SAYS**

For accurate piecing, it is of paramount importance that you sew an accurate ¼″ seam allowance.

Cutting strips

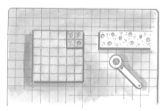

Cutting squares

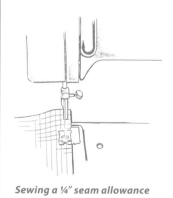

Sewing a ¼″ seam allowance

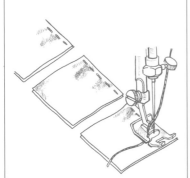

Chain piecing

first set of pieces that are to be sewn together right sides facing with raw edges even. Stitch the seam, guiding the pieces along the edge of the presser foot or masking tape. At the end of the seam, stop sewing. Without lifting the presser foot or cutting the threads, feed the next set of patches into the machine right after the first set. Continue in this manner feeding patches into the machine forming a chain. When they are all sewn, clip the threads between the pieces. That was fast!

Appliqué

All of the appliqué projects in *Quilting with Jodie in Cotton Country* are made through a simple cut-and-fuse method using a double-stick fusible web such as Steam-a-Seam II®. If you wish, you may use the traditional needle turn appliqué instead.

TRANSFERRING DESIGNS

Whether you appliqué by hand, by machine, or by fusing, the first step is to transfer the template designs onto the fabrics you plan to cut them from. Tape the pattern to a window and tape the fabric you wish to mark over the top of it. Use a disappearing marker or a washable marker to trace the design. (I prefer the Crayola brand, but test your marker first to make sure it washes out.) If you have one, use the same technique on a light-board.

FUSIBLE APPLIQUÉ

First, be sure to read through the manufacturer's direction that are packaged with the brand of fusible web you choose and take note of any special steps that are recommended there.

1. Copy the patterns from the book and trace them onto one side of the double-stick fusible web. Cut out the shape roughly, leaving about ½″ of fabric outside the drawn lines.

2. Being careful to leave the web in place, remove the unmarked paper only and stick the fusible web to the wrong side of the fabric. You may finger press or use an iron.

3. Cut through all layers along the marked lines.

4. Peel off the remaining, marked paper and stick the appliqué in place onto your quilt block or sewing project. Once you have all of the pieces in place and are happy with the arrangement, press for 10 to 15 seconds, as directed by manufacturer.

5. To secure the edges of your appliqué shapes, you may blanket stitch them by hand or use a machine satin stitch. The projects in *Quilting with Jodie in Cotton Country* use both methods.

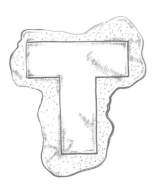

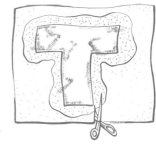

Step 1

Step 3

Hand embroidery

Embroidery

Two types of embroidery are used in *Quilting with Jodie in Cotton Country*. For the appliqué quilt projects, the designs are fused using double-stick fusible web, then the edges are secured using either a hand or machine blanket stitch. Embroidered projects use several stitches which are easy for the beginner to master. My favorite embroidery floss is made by DMC® and is widely available at crafts and sewing stores. For machine embroidery, I use many different brands of thread, including Mettler and Sulky.

HAND EMBROIDERY DIRECTIONS

Cut an 18″ length of floss. Separate the floss one strand at a time by grasping the tip of one strand and pulling up from the group, as shown. Thread the needle with two strands.

Starting and Ending

To start, put a knot in the thread and enter the fabric from the wrong side, thereby leaving the knot hidden at the back. To end, simply slide the needle under an inch of worked stitches on the wrong side and cut the thread.

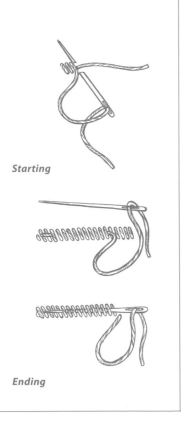

Starting

Ending

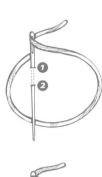
Running stitch

Chain stitch

Running Stitch

Enter from the back then weave the needle through the fabric, making even stitches that are longer than the spaces between them.

Chain Stitch

Enter from the back and come up at the desired start point at the front. To form a loop, hold the thread down with your thumb, go down at 1 (as close as possible to your start point), and come back up at 2, with the needle tip over the thread. Repeat along the marked line, forming a chain of stitches.

Blanket Stitch

Come up at point 1. Holding the thread down with your thumb, go down at 2 and come back up at 3 with the needle tip over the thread. Pull the stitch into place. Repeat, stitching so the bottom "legs" of the stitch form an outline along the raw edge of the appliqué shape.

MACHINE EMBROIDERY DIRECTIONS

Test your machine's blanket stitch on scrap fabric, as the standard setting may or may not be the right size for your project. The "straight" part of the stitch should be as close to the cut edge of the appliqué as possible, thereby positioning the "zigzag" part of the stitch on the appliqué.

To stitch around shapes, leave the needle in the fabric as you pivot the project, and then continue sewing. (For excellent instruction in machine appliqué, look for *Mastering Machine Appliqué* by Harriet Hargrave.)

❝ JODIE SAYS

To keep "ghost" threads (the tails of knots) from showing through to the front, weave them into the stitches on the back. This way, the back of the work will be as neat as the front. ❞

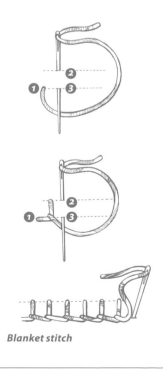
Blanket stitch

> **❝ JODIE SAYS**
> When hand quilting your thread will often twist from constant needle action. To remedy, drop the needle and let it dangle freely until the thread unwinds. **❞**

Assembly and Finishing

LAYERING THE QUILT "SANDWICH"

Before you quilt your quilt, you must assemble the three layers (top, batting and backing) and secure them to prevent slipping during quilting.

1. Press the quilt top and the backing. Lay the backing on your work surface and smooth it. Use masking tape to secure the edges.

2. Place the batting on top of the backing, smoothing it in place.

3. Lay the quilt top, right side up, on top of the batting.

4. Secure the layers together by either basting them or safety pinning. The stitches or pins should be 4″ to 6″ apart.

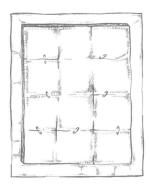

Layering the quilt "sandwich"

Quilting

HAND QUILTING

Quilting stitches are simply short running stitches worked from the top of the quilt. Quilting holds the layers of the quilt together.

1. Tie a single knot in an 18″ length of quilting thread. Insert the needle into the quilt top and emerge where you wish to start stitching. Tug on the thread to lodge the knot in the batting.

2. Take a backstitch and begin quilting, making a small running stitch through all layers. Take several straight and even stitches at a time.

3. To end a line of quilting, make a knot in the thread near the quilt top. Take a small backstitch, running the needle into the batting and back out the quilt top. Tug on the thread to lodge the needle in the batting. Trim the thread.

MACHINE QUILTING

To quilt straight lines by machine, use a walking foot. A walking foot helps to feed the layers of the quilt evenly, thereby preventing puckers. As an added benefit, your stitches will be even.

For free-motion work, outline quilting, stippling swirls, or meander quilting, use a darning foot and lower the feed dogs of your machine. This requires practice.

To learn more about hand or machine quilting, invest in one or more books on the subject and check with your local quilt shop to take a class. My suggestions for great books on the subject can be found in the Bookshelf section on page 96.

Binding

1. Cut the fabric into 2½″-wide strips. Stitch the binding strips together on the diagonal, end to end, to form a continuous strip. Press the seams open. Press the binding in half lengthwise so the wrong sides are facing.

2. Trim the batting and backing even with the quilt top. Place the binding strip along one edge of the right side of the quilt top, matching raw edges. Leaving the first 4″ or so free, stitch the binding to the quilt. Use a ¼″ seam allowance. Stop stitching ¼″ from the corner. Backstitch and remove the quilt from the machine.

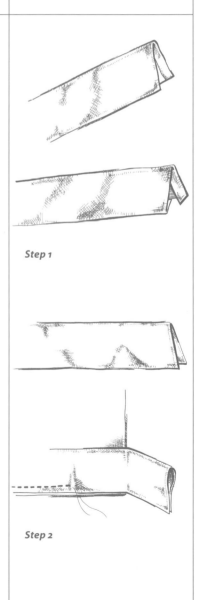

Step 1

Step 2

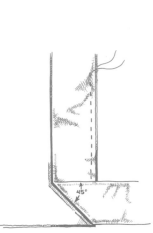

Step 3

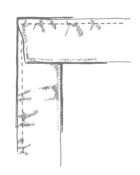

Step 4

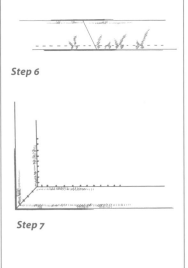

Step 6

Step 7

3. Turn the quilt to prepare for sewing the next edge. Fold the binding up, creating a 45° angle fold. Fold the binding down, making the fold even with the top edge of the quilt and the raw edge aligned with the side of the quilt.

4. Beginning at the edge, stitch the binding to the quilt, stopping ¼″ from the next corner.

5. Backstitch and remove the quilt from the machine. Continue the folding and stitching process for the remaining corners.

6. When you are within approximately 4″ of the starting point, stop stitching. Cut the binding end so it overlaps the unstitched binding at the beginning by at about 2″. Cut the end diagonally. Turn the diagonal edge under ¼″ and insert the beginning end inside the fold. Finish sewing the binding to the quilt.

7. Fold the binding to the back of the quilt over the raw edges of the quilt sandwich, covering the machine stitching. A miter will appear on the front. Whipstitch the binding to the back of the quilt.

Hanging Sleeve

1. Cut a strip of fabric 6″ to 8″ wide and 1″ to 2″ shorter than the width of the quilt at the top edge. To hem the short ends, press under ¼″ twice and topstitch.

2. Fold the fabric strip in half lengthwise, wrong sides facing. Seam the long raw edges together using a ¼″ seam allowance. Fold the tube so that the seam is centered on one side and press the seam allowances open.

3. Pin the tube to the back of the quilt, just below the binding, with the seamed side against the quilt. Hand-sew the top edge of the sleeve to the quilt backing.

4. Push the tube up so the top edge covers about half of the binding. Pin and sew the bottom edge of the sleeve to the quilt backing. This will provide some give to accommodate the hanging rod.

5. To hang your quilt, insert a curtain rod or wooden dowel into the sleeve and suspend the quilt on brackets. Or attach screw eyes or drill holes in the ends of a length of lathe and slip the eyes or holes over small nails in the wall.

Step 1

Step 2

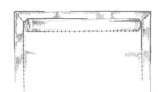

Step 3

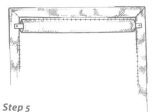

Step 4

Step 5

Quilt Label

Whether you give your project as a gift or keep it for yourself, be sure future caretakers know from whence your creation came. Here's an easy label for you to print onto fabric, personalize, and attach to the back of your project.

Using an ink jet printer—I use an HP all-in-one that does a remarkable job of rendering wonderful color and its many capabilities are handy in my studio—and special printable fabric (available from quilting and craft stores), transfer the label image to the printable fabric. Then personalize the label using a Pigma Micron Pen.

1. Place a sheet of printable fabric in the paper tray of your printer. Place the book on the copier glass. Press print.

2. Personalize the label using a permanent pen.

3. Cut along the marked lines.

4. To apply to your quilt, you may fuse with fusible web and blanket stitch the edges, or turn under the edges ¼″ and hand stitch the label in place.

Templates

Cabin in the Field *see page 4*

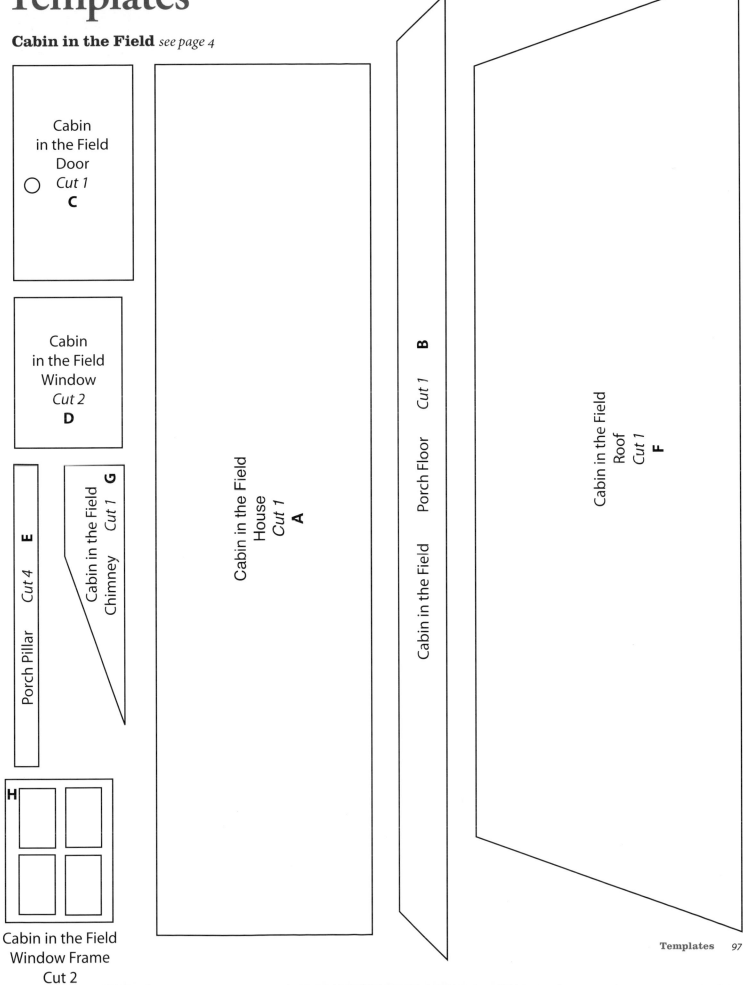

Cabin
in the Field
Door
Cut 1
C

Cabin
in the Field
Window
Cut 2
D

Cabin in the Field
Chimney   *Cut 1*   **G**

Porch Pillar   *Cut 4*   **E**

H

Cabin in the Field
Window Frame
Cut 2

Cabin in the Field
House
Cut 1
A

Cabin in the Field   Porch Floor   *Cut 1*   **B**

Cabin in the Field
Roof
Cut 1
F

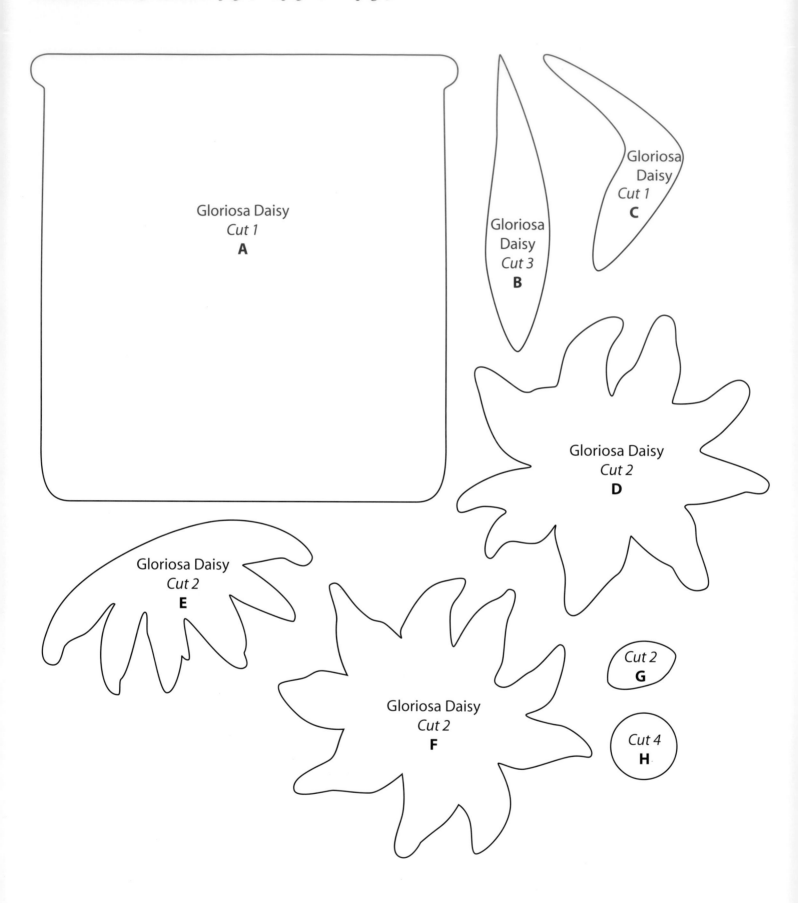

Gloriosa Daisy
Cut 1
A

Gloriosa
Daisy
Cut 3
B

Gloriosa
Daisy
Cut 1
C

Gloriosa Daisy
Cut 2
D

Gloriosa Daisy
Cut 2
E

Gloriosa Daisy
Cut 2
F

Cut 2
G

Cut 4
H

Trio of Mules: Center Mule *see page 5*

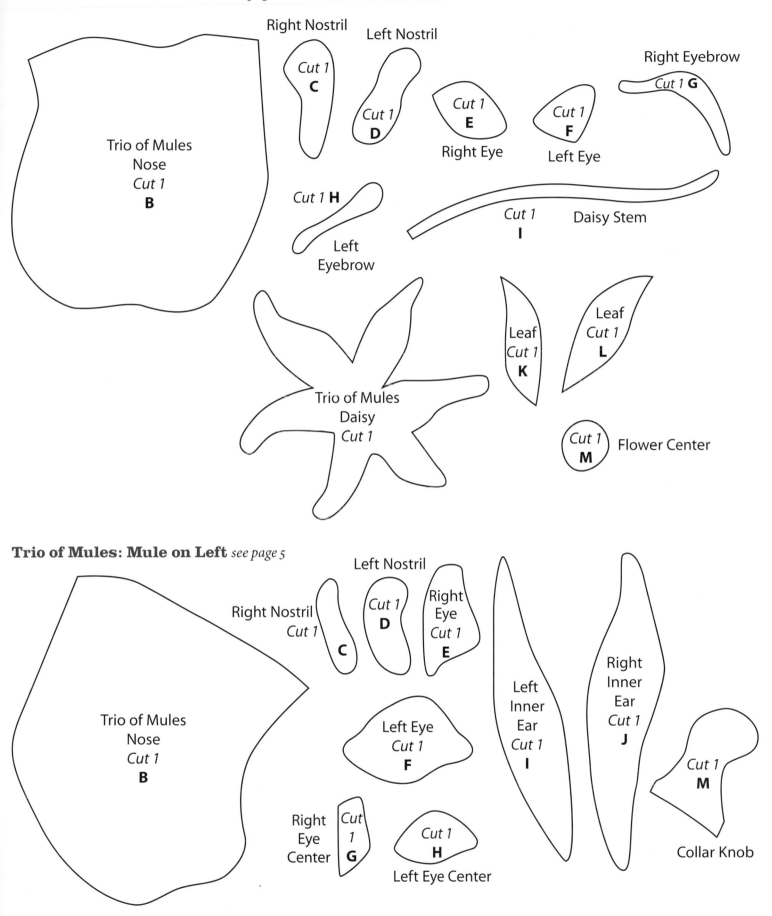

Right Nostril

Cut 1
C

Left Nostril

Cut 1
D

Cut 1
E
Right Eye

Cut 1
F
Left Eye

Right Eyebrow

Cut 1 **G**

Trio of Mules
Nose
Cut 1
B

Cut 1 **H**

Left
Eyebrow

Cut 1
I
Daisy Stem

Leaf
Cut 1
K

Leaf
Cut 1
L

Trio of Mules
Daisy
Cut 1

Cut 1
M
Flower Center

Trio of Mules: Mule on Left *see page 5*

Left Nostril

Cut 1
D

Right
Eye
Cut 1
E

Right Nostril

Cut 1

C

Trio of Mules
Nose
Cut 1
B

Left Eye
Cut 1
F

Left
Inner
Ear
Cut 1
I

Right
Inner
Ear
Cut 1
J

Cut 1
M

Right
Eye
Center

Cut 1
G

Cut 1
H

Left Eye Center

Collar Knob

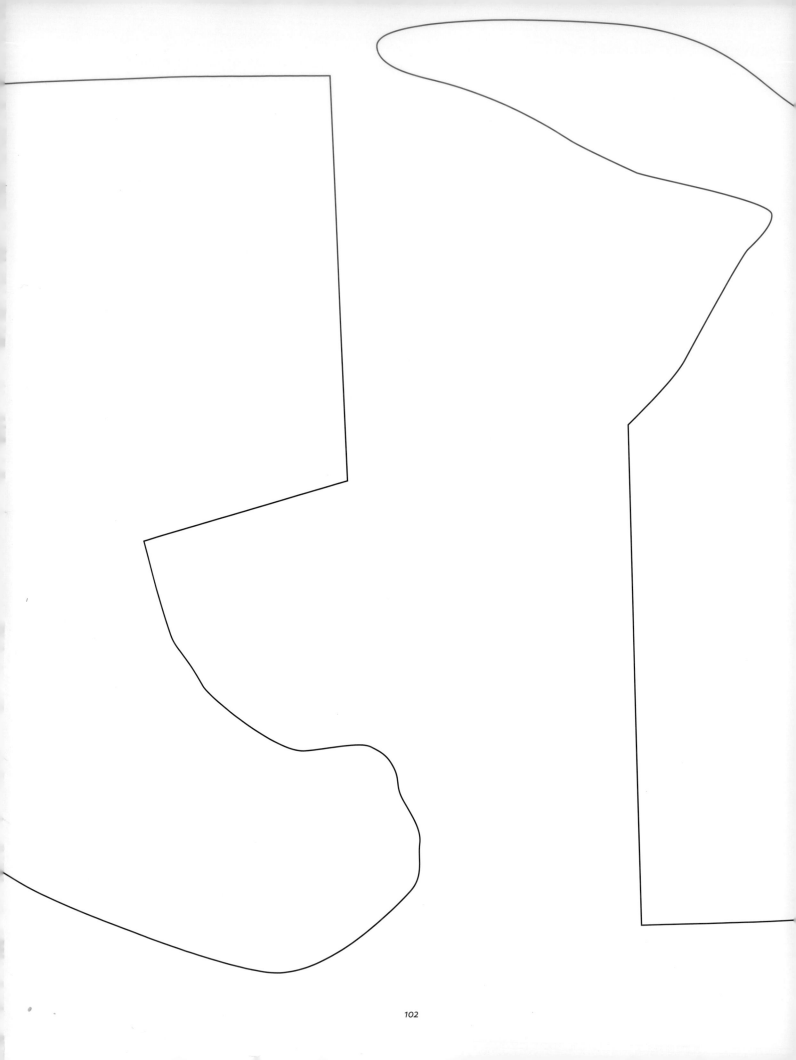

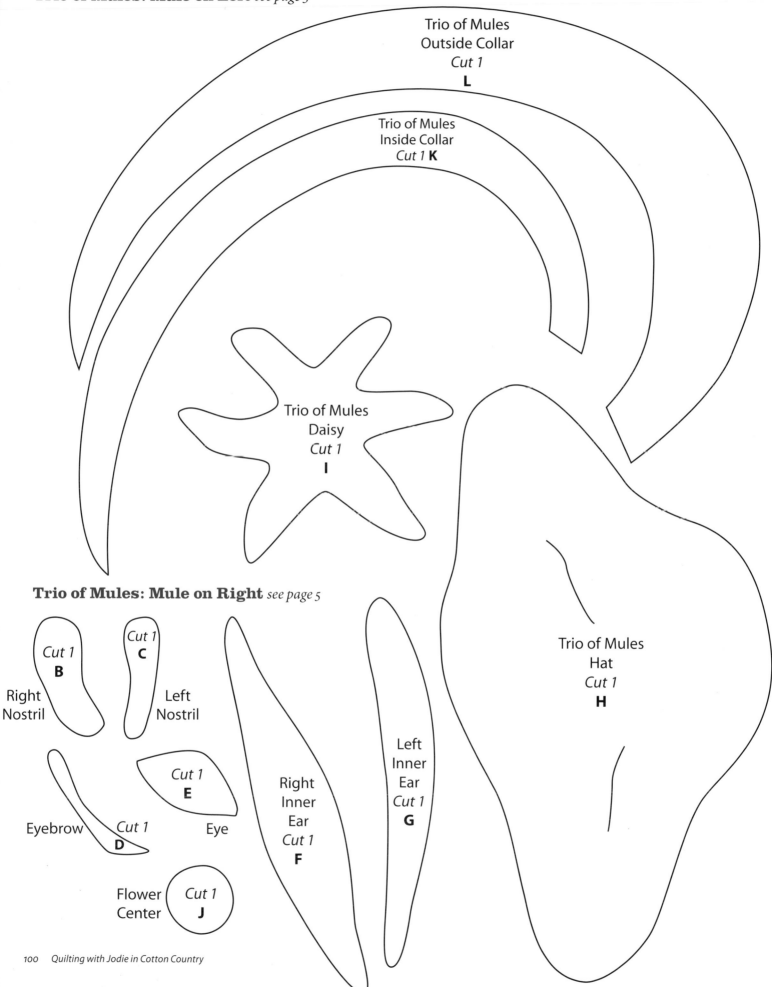

Trio of Mules
Outside Collar
Cut 1
L

Trio of Mules
Inside Collar
Cut 1 **K**

Trio of Mules
Daisy
Cut 1
I

Trio of Mules: Mule on Right *see page 5*

Cut 1
B

Right
Nostril

Cut 1
C

Left
Nostril

Cut 1
E

Eye

Cut 1
D

Eyebrow

Right
Inner
Ear
Cut 1
F

Left
Inner
Ear
Cut 1
G

Trio of Mules
Hat
Cut 1
H

Flower
Center

Cut 1
J

Trio of Mules
Mule on Left
Cut 1
A

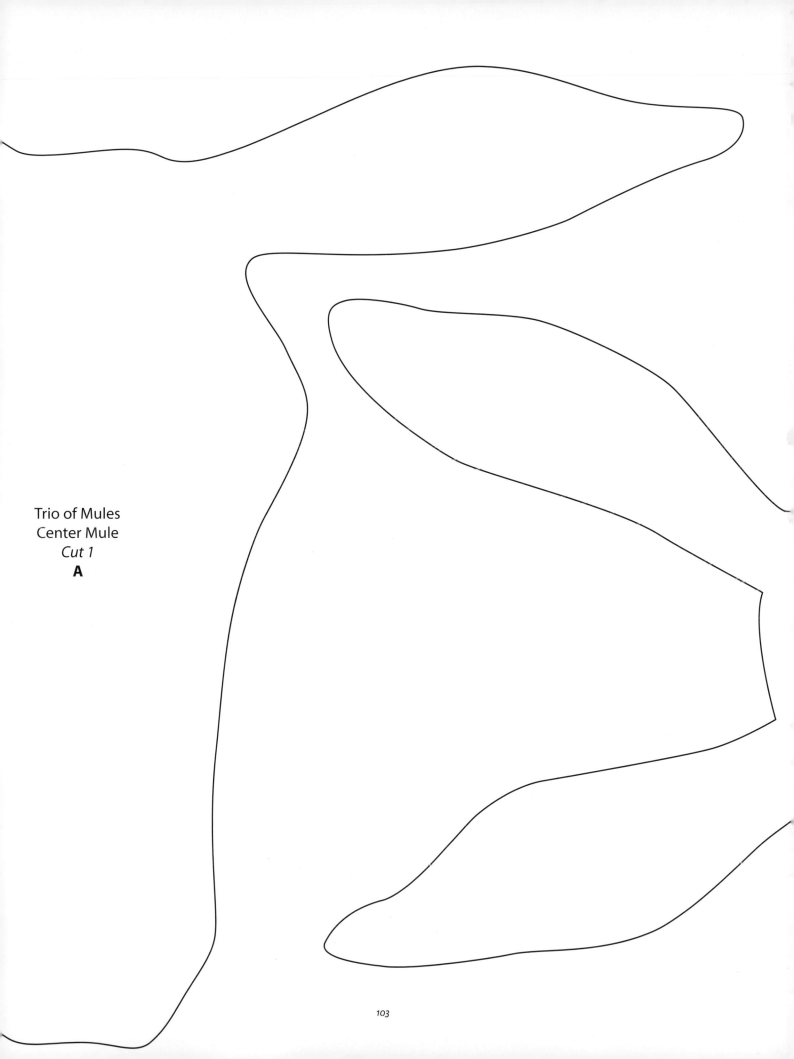

Trio of Mules
Center Mule
Cut 1
A

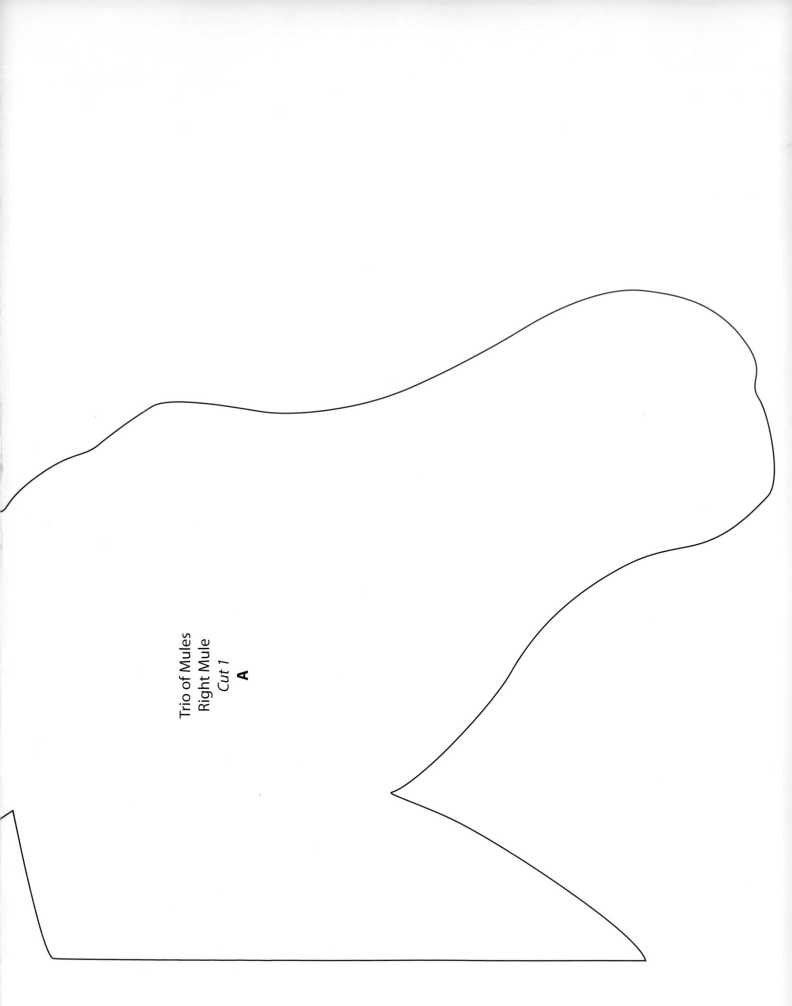

Trio of Mules
Right Mule
Cut 1
A

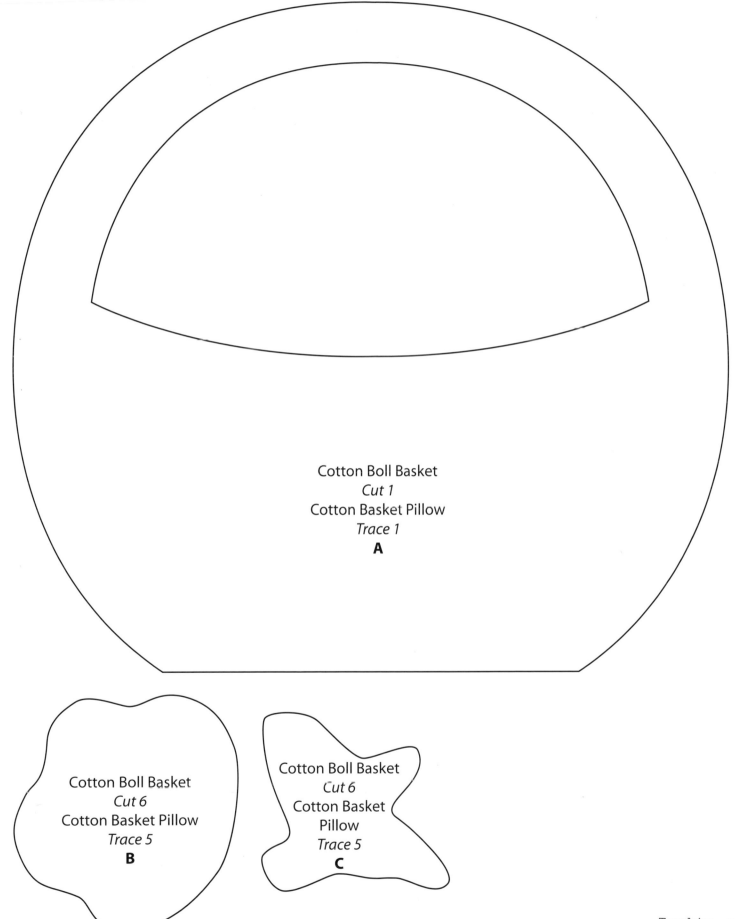

Cotton Boll Basket
Cut 1
Cotton Basket Pillow
Trace 1
A

Cotton Boll Basket
Cut 6
Cotton Basket Pillow
Trace 5
B

Cotton Boll Basket
Cut 6
Cotton Basket
Pillow
Trace 5
C

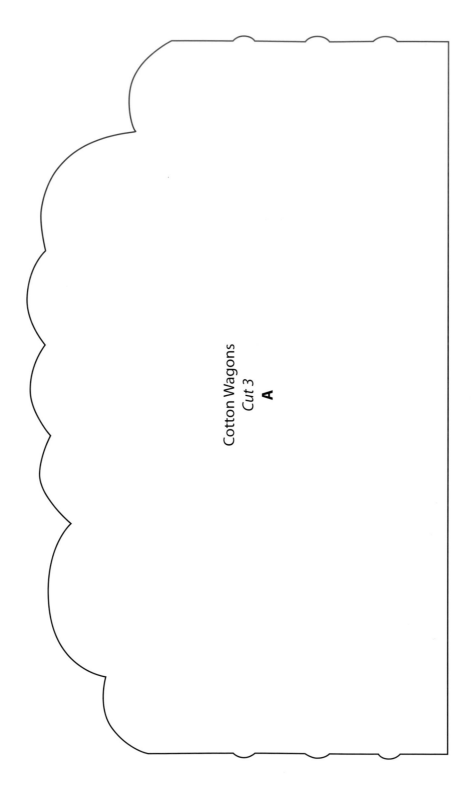

Cotton Wagons
Cut 3
A

Cotton Wagons Block *see page 6*

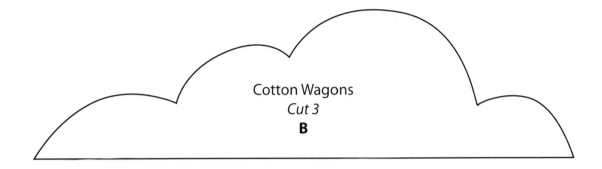

Cotton Wagons
Cut 3
B

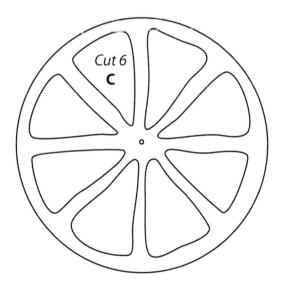

Cut 6
C

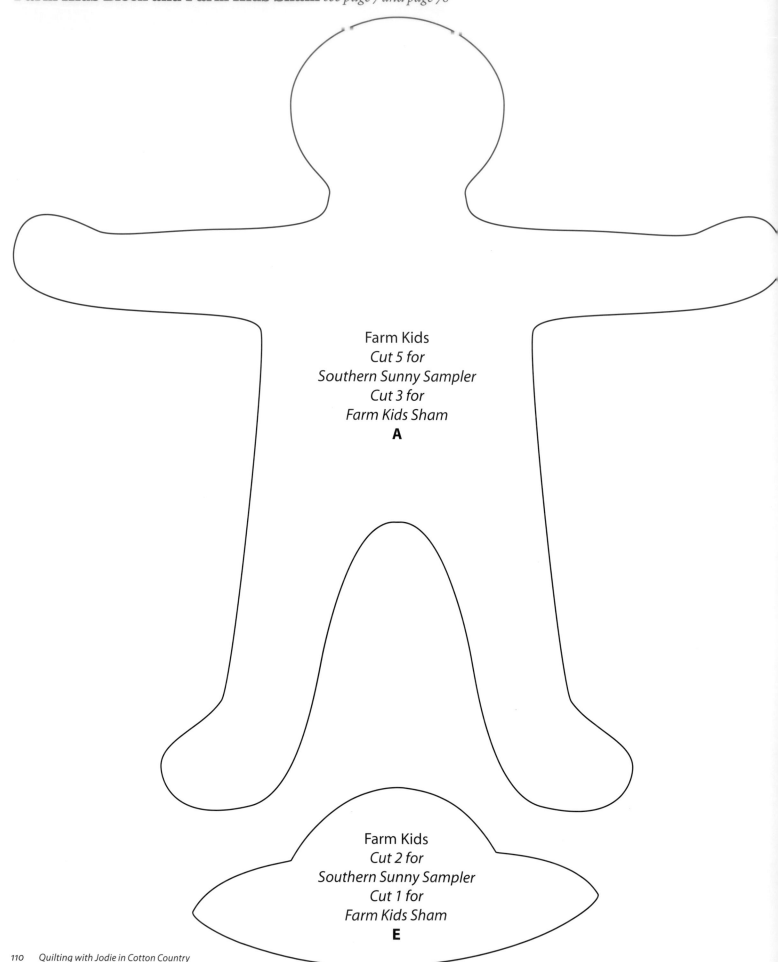

Farm Kids
Cut 5 for
Southern Sunny Sampler
Cut 3 for
Farm Kids Sham
A

Farm Kids
Cut 2 for
Southern Sunny Sampler
Cut 1 for
Farm Kids Sham
E

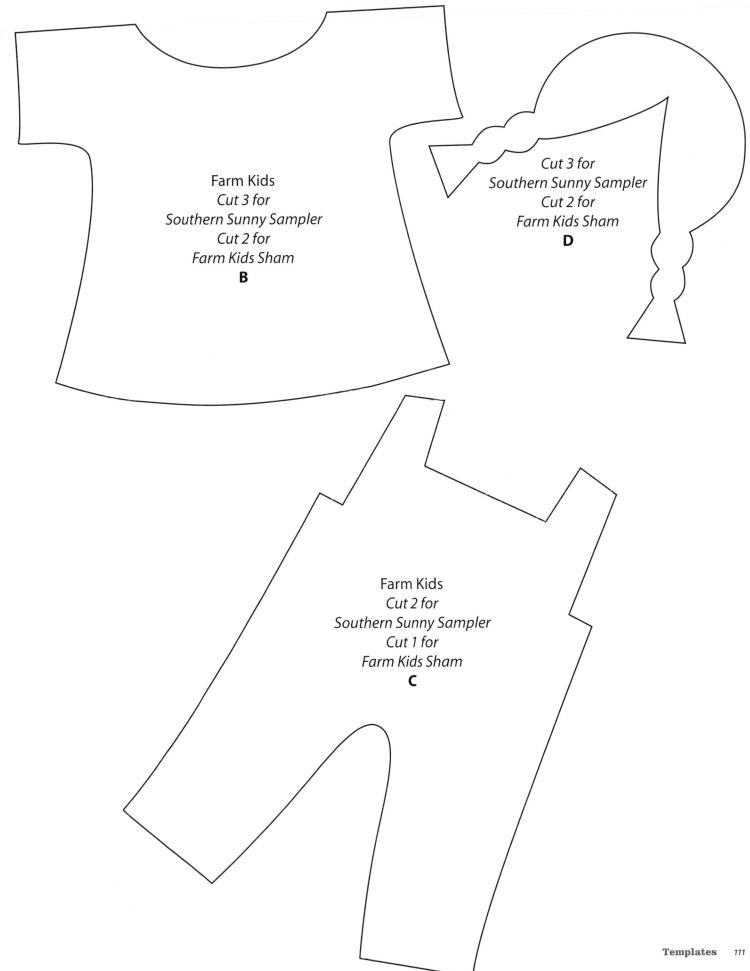

Farm Kids
Cut 3 for
Southern Sunny Sampler
Cut 2 for
Farm Kids Sham
B

Cut 3 for
Southern Sunny Sampler
Cut 2 for
Farm Kids Sham
D

Farm Kids
Cut 2 for
Southern Sunny Sampler
Cut 1 for
Farm Kids Sham
C

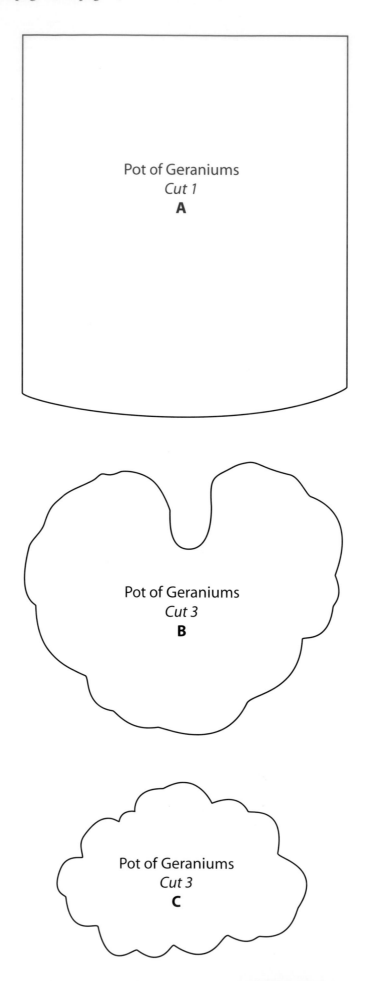

Pot of Geraniums
Cut 1
A

Pot of Geraniums
Cut 3
B

Pot of Geraniums
Cut 3
C

Sweet Iced Tea Block *see page 10 and page 25*

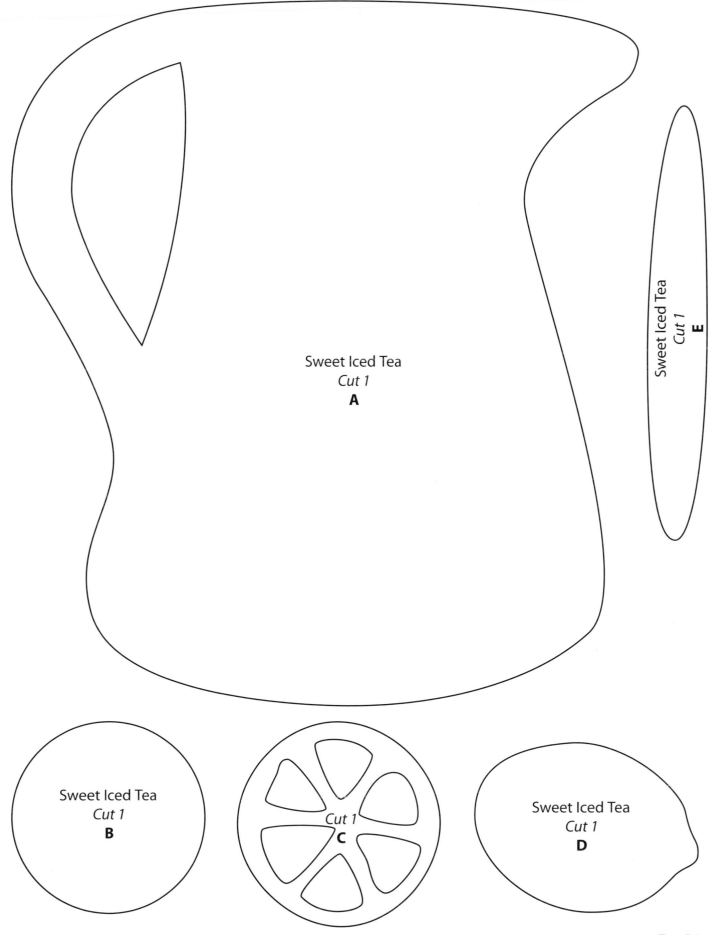

Sweet Iced Tea
Cut 1
A

Sweet Iced Tea
Cut 1
E

Sweet Iced Tea
Cut 1
B

Cut 1
C

Sweet Iced Tea
Cut 1
D

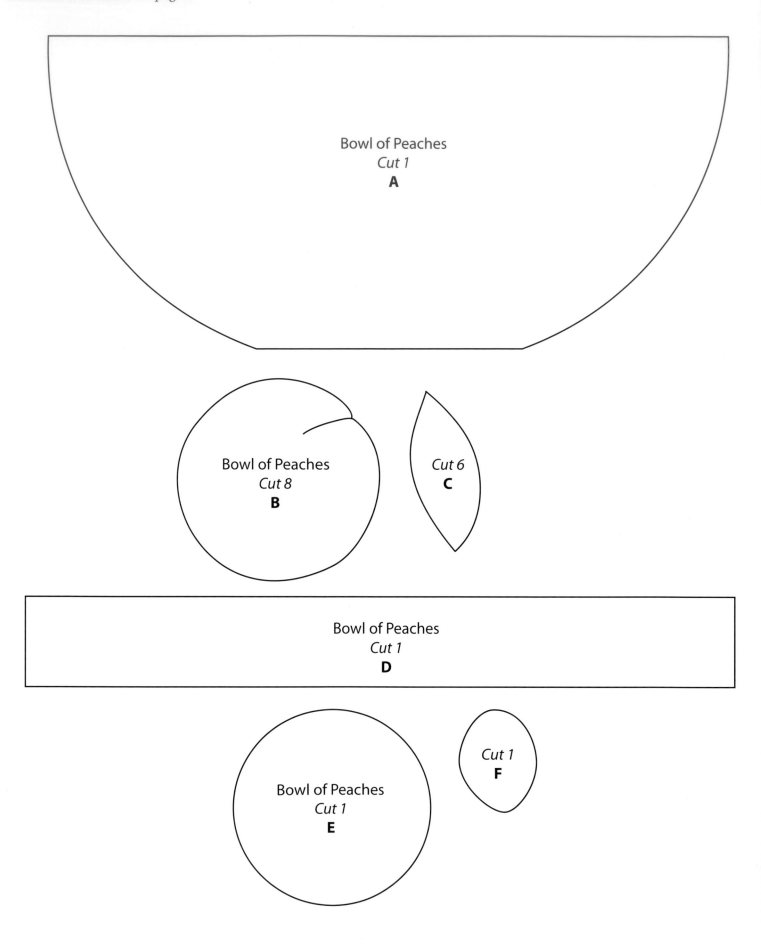

Bowl of Peaches
Cut 1
A

Bowl of Peaches
Cut 8
B

Cut 6
C

Bowl of Peaches
Cut 1
D

Bowl of Peaches
Cut 1
E

Cut 1
F

Peach Jam
Cut 1
C

Peach Jam
Cut 1
A

Cut 1
B

PEACH JAM

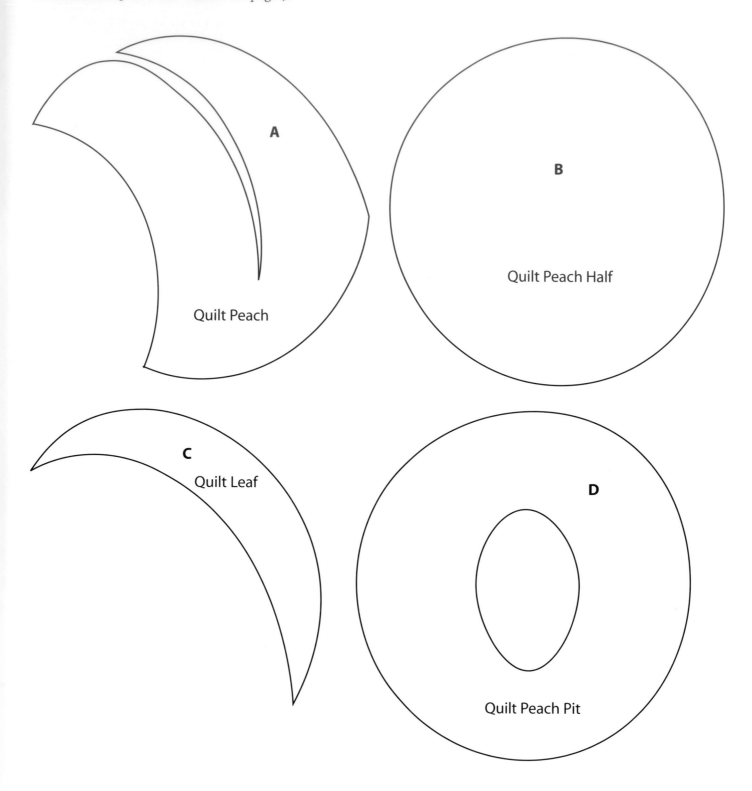

A

Quilt Peach

B

Quilt Peach Half

C

Quilt Leaf

D

Quilt Peach Pit

Summer Placemats *see page 47*

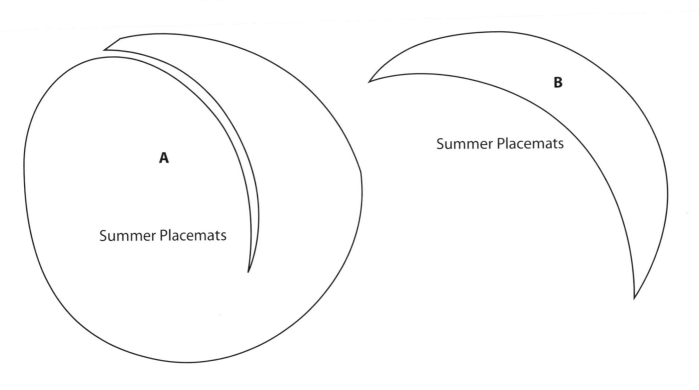

A

Summer Placemats

B

Summer Placemats

Redwork Cotton Boll Pillow and Lap Quilt *see pages 57 and 59*

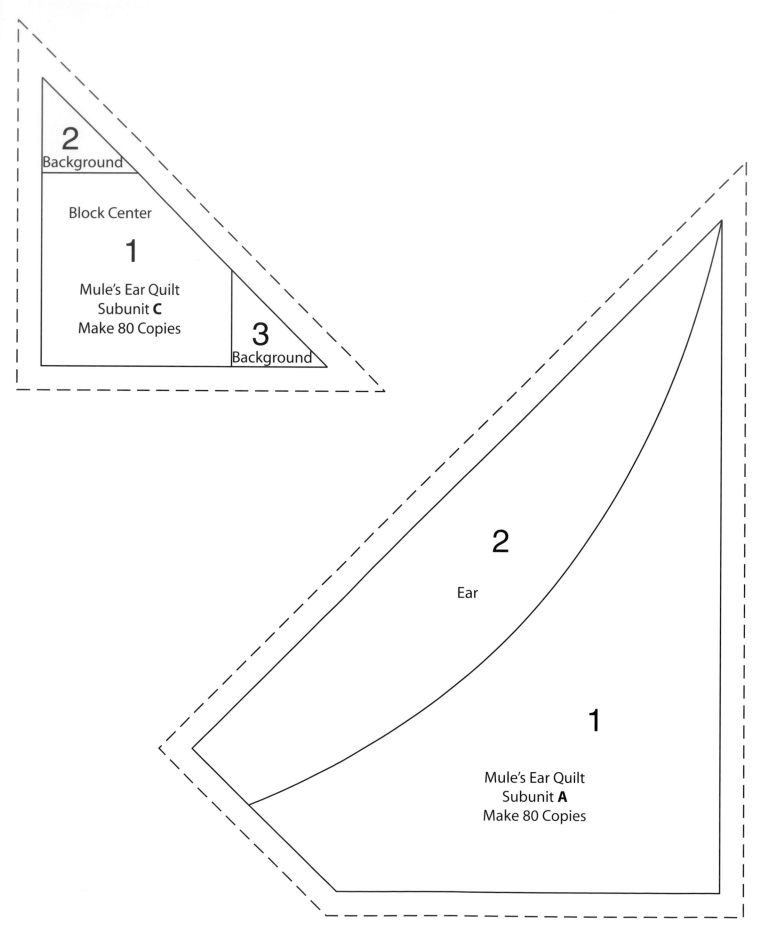

2
Background

Block Center

1

Mule's Ear Quilt
Subunit **C**
Make 80 Copies

3
Background

2

Ear

1

Mule's Ear Quilt
Subunit **A**
Make 80 Copies

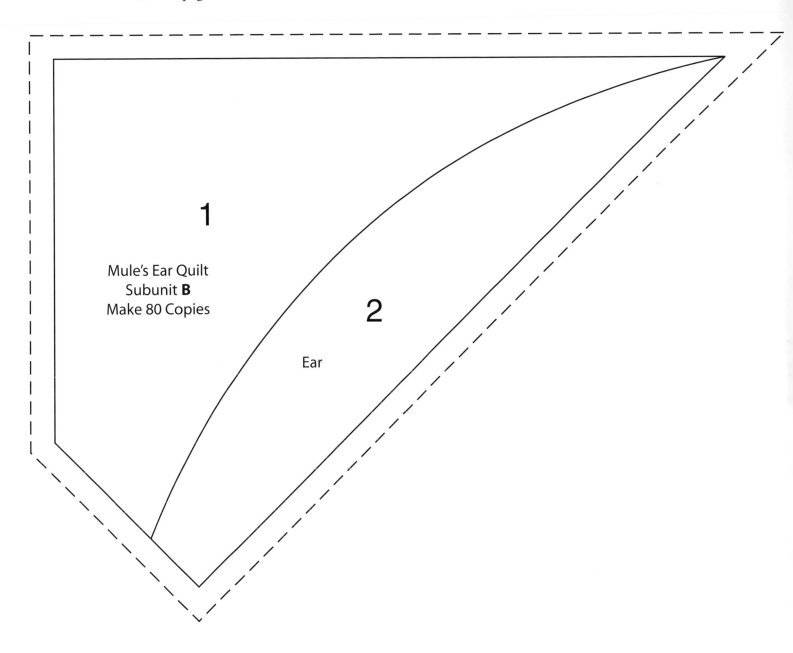

1

Mule's Ear Quilt
Subunit **B**
Make 80 Copies

2

Ear

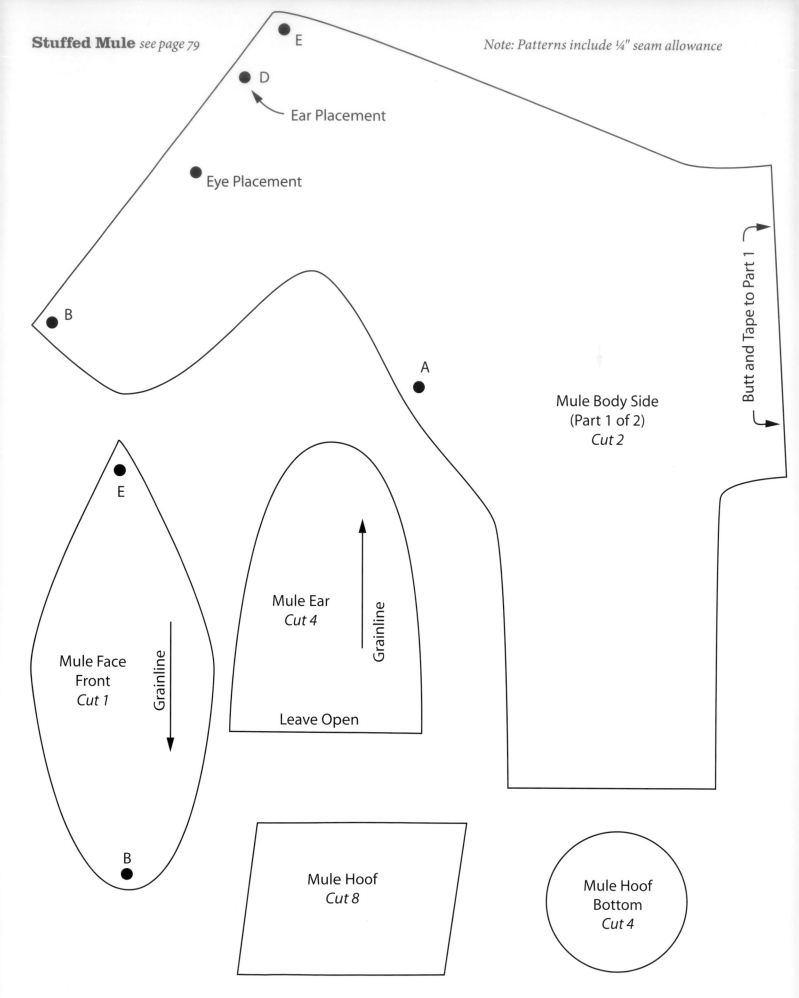

Note: Patterns include ¼" seam allowance

E

D

Ear Placement

Eye Placement

B

A

Mule Body Side
(Part 1 of 2)
Cut 2

Butt and Tape to Part 1

E

Mule Ear
Cut 4

Grainline

Mule Face
Front
Cut 1

Grainline

Leave Open

B

Mule Hoof
Cut 8

Mule Hoof
Bottom
Cut 4

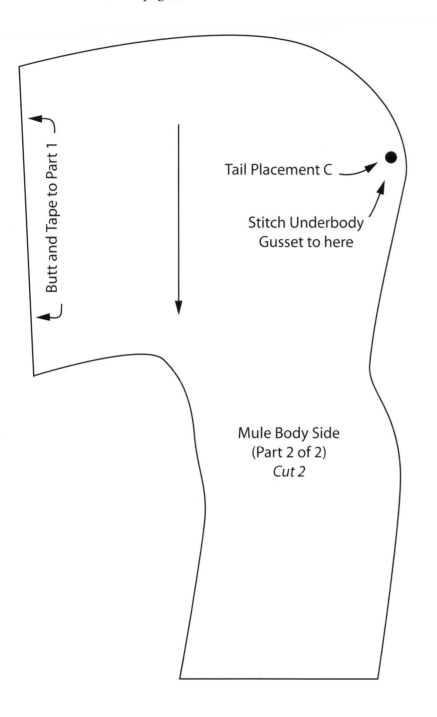

Butt and Tape to Part 1

Tail Placement C

Stitch Underbody
Gusset to here

Mule Body Side
(Part 2 of 2)
Cut 2

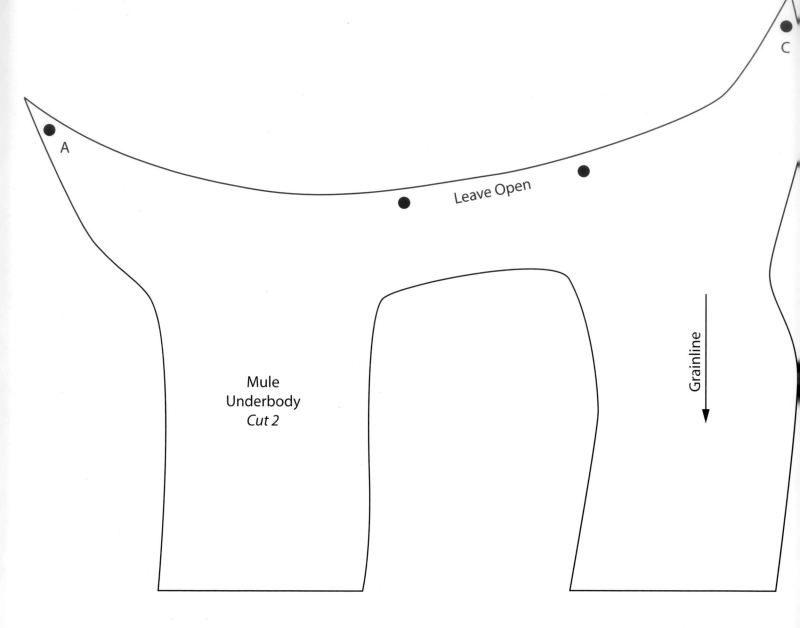

Leave Open

A

C

Mule
Underbody
Cut 2

Grainline